ROGUE PUBLISHER

à Orsay, ???
18. July 1845

ROGUE PUBLISHER
THE 'PRINCE OF PUFFERS'
The Life and Works of the Publisher
Henry Colburn

John Sutherland
and
Veronica Melnyk

EER
Edward Edward Root, Publishers, Brighton, 2018.

EER
Edward Everett Root, Publishers, Co. Ltd.,
30 New Road, Brighton, Sussex, BN1 1BN, England.
www.eerpublishing.com

edwardeverettroot@yahoo.co.uk

Rogue Publisher
The 'Prince of Puffers'
The Life and Works of the Publisher Henry Colburn

John Sutherland and Veronica Melnyk

First published in England 2018.
© John Sutherland and Veronica Melnyk 2018.
This edition © Edward Everett Root Publishers 2018.

ISBN: 9781911204558 Hardback
ISBN: 9781011204947 e-book

Design by Pageset Limited, High Wycombe, Buckinghamshire.
Printed in Great Britain by Lightning Source UK, Milton Keynes.

"Henry Colburn revolutionised publishing in its every aspect".

– Michael Sadleir

CONTENTS

ILLUSTRATIONS

Some of the books issued by Colburn and Bentley.

The plates: Charles Lever, *Arthur O'Leary*. Benjamin
Disraeli, *Coningsby*. Lady Morgan, *Florence Macarthy*.
R.S. Surtees, *Handley Cross*. Victoire, Count de
Soligny, *Letters on England*. Mrs. C. Gore, *Women As
They Are*. M. de Bourienne, *The Life of Napoleon*. *The
New Monthly Magazine*. *Colburn's Standard Novels*.
Colburn's Standard Novelists. *Colburn's Modern Novelists*.
G.E. Jewsbury, *Marian Walters*. B. Disraeli, *Lord George
Bentinck, a Political Biography*. *The Literary Gazette*.
New Monthly Magazine. Mrs. C. Gore, *Men of Capital*.
Colburn's Modern Novelists. Mrs. C. Gore, *Mothers and
Daughters*. Mrs. C. Gore, *Mrs. Armytage; or, Female
Domination*. Bulwer-Lytton, *Pelham*. Mrs. C. Gore, *Pin
Money*. Mrs. C. Gore, *Preferment*. Colonel Lach Szyrma
(ed.), *Revelations of Siberia*. Lady Morgan, *O'Donnell; A
National Tale*. Baroness de Stael-Holstein, *Memoirs of
the Private Life of My Father*. William Bray (ed.), *Diary
and Correspondence of John Evelyn, FRS*. Victoire, Count
de Soligny, *Letters on England*. *Bentley's Standard Novels*.
Lady Morgan (portrait).

Original autograph letter dated July 19 1842 from
13 Great Marlborough St to J B Burke signed by H.
Colburn. Original autograph letter dated 'Monday'
from London to Mrs Samuel Carter Hall signed by
H Colburn. Original autograph letter dated July 19
1842 from 13 Great Marlborough St to J B Burke
signed by H. Colburn, and Original autograph letter
dated 'Monday' from London to Mrs Samuel Carter
Hall signed by H Colburn.

PREFACE: WHO WAS HENRY COLBURN?

Henry Colburn is not a name that rings loudly in the annals of nineteenth-century literature. On the face of it, that invisibility is unsurprising. Publishers—the mere coat-brushers of books, as Thomas Carlyle called them—rarely hog any spotlight that's going. Nonetheless their input is formative: on the authors they choose to bring forward into the market ('literary gatekeepers' would be a kinder description than Carlyle's); on the reading public whose preferences they respond to; and, most importantly, in their control of the complex apparatus of the book-trade and literary world.

However legend portrays him, Henry Colburn was, incontrovertibly, one of the prime movers in the British publishing world at the historical moment when it was moving into its recognizably modern shape. One should go a step further and call him one of the shapers of what our book-world now is.

And yet, if posterity remembers Henry Colburn at all, it is as a blot on the fair name of British publishing, which was, and is, dominated at its top tier by 'gentlemanly' dynasties—the Blackwoods, Murrays, Macmillans, the great university duopoly, OUP / CUP—all mingling with the power elite of the state. (The Macmillan dynasty—having introduced the Net Book Agreement, which organized the British book trade for a century—supplied Britain with the Prime Minister who oversaw the dismantling of the British Empire. The Macmillan firm, ironically, had been

Yours faithfully,

T. Carlyle.

TRANSLATOR OF "WILHELM MEISTER"

for decades notably enriched by its 'colonial' editions.)[1]

If there is a louse on the locks of literature, booklore tells us, it is Henry Colburn. Or so we are led to believe. This Janus-like contradiction in Colburn's image is a paradox which has attracted the two authors of this book (with an obligato from their publisher, John Spiers).

Veronica Melnyk has written the only full-length scholarly thesis on Henry Colburn and his business, turning up, in the process, a wealth of hitherto unexamined primary information. The material was not easily found, and took years to uncover. Hers is the solid foundation on which what follows mainly rests.[2] She calls, in her thesis and in this book, for a radical (and more sympathetic) reappraisal of posterity's thinking about Henry Colburn.

John Sutherland has had a long-standing interest in publishing history (which few academics, sadly, share) and an equally long-standing curiosity about Colburn, and the nineteenth-century fiction, particularly popular fiction, which was Colburn's main stock in trade.

Professor John Spiers is a scholar, bibliophile and publisher (of this book, among others). No one knows the feel and look of Colburn's physical product better than Professor Spiers. Fuller biographical profiles of the three of us can be found at the end of the book.

The driving force behind the book, the reason for writing it, is fascination with this shadowy, strangely potent, elusive giant of the book world of his day—a long day from the early Regency to the Victorian heyday of the mid-fifties. The aim of the book is to see Henry Colburn clear.

---

[1] See *Macmillan: A Publishing Tradition, 1843–1970,* Ed. Elizabeth E. James (Palgrave, 2002).

[2] For Melnyk's account of the sketchy, often contradictory or ill-informed sources, which have in many cases been drawn on carelessly, and what they can nonetheless supply, see, "'Half fashion and half passion': The Life of Publisher Henry Colburn". Ph.D. thesis, University of Birmingham. 2002, http://etheses.bham.ac.uk/163/.

HENRY COLBURN: THE CHARGE SHEET

Literary and publishing history have drawn up a formidable charge sheet against Henry Colburn. In personal pedigree he is slandered as a 'guttersnipe', or a 'royal bastard'.[3] His natal origins are impenetrably obscure—probably murky. Various rumours circulated in his day that he was either an illegitimate child of the Duke of York or of Lord Landsdowne.[4] Date uncertain. It pleased Colburn to weave illustrious (typically mendacious) pedigrees for himself as blithely as he did for the dubiously aristocratic purveyors of his silver fork novels. Mystique was one of his promotional devices. It tickled reader appetites and sent his wares flying off the shelves.

In his dealings with authors, Colburn was, as Mrs. Gore

---

[3] See Matthew W. Rosa, *The Silver Fork School* (New York, 1936), p. 179.

[4] The Duke of York and Albany (1763–1827), is famous from the 'Grand Old Duke of York' nursery rhyme. He was the second son, and favourite, of George III. He took up a military career of dubious success on the field of battle; but he did set up Sandhurst Military College. He had numerous mistresses. One, Mary Anne Clarke, had connections in the book world—but her date of birth, 1776, is too late for her to have been Colburn's mother. William Petty, the 1st Marquess of Lansdowne (2 May 1737–7 May 1805) was prime minister during the last months of the American War of Independence. One's suspicion is that the ascription of Colburn's parentage to these grand figures originated, covertly, with Colburn himself.

put it, Scylla to his erstwhile partner Richard Bentley's Charybdis.[5] A mortal threat to the honest author. Or—in Disraeli's more pungent description—he was a publishing 'bawd', engaged in wholesale literary prostitution.[6] Disraeli, one may note (see below), owed his career as a novelist to Colburn; and his career as a politician hinged on his career as a novelist.[7] Dickens, who published one book with Colburn (a charitable volume, pro bono, designed for the relief of the family of another publisher, John Macrone) described Colburn as a 'sneaking vagabond'[8] who conducted business like a pawnbroker on Saturday night. Dickens never had a high opinion of publishers. Colburn was, in the Great Inimitable's opinion, the pits.

Harriet Martineau said that dealing with Colburn made her feel as if she were on the block at a slave market.[9] Violated. Colburn, said the novelist Charles Lever, with a manlier flight of contempt, ordered novels from novelists (even those with a name, like the author of *Harry Lorrequer*) as someone might order breeches from their tailor.[10]

At times Colburn's malefactions verged on the criminal.[11] Just before his death, in 1855, acting as an agent for a fellow

---

[5] M. Oliphant, *Annals of a Publishing House* (Edinburgh, 1897), Vol II, p. 349.

[6] Robert Blake, *Disraeli* (London, 1966), p. 55.

[7] For Disraeli's connection with Colburn, see B. R. Jerman, 'The Production of Disraeli's Trilogy', PBSA, Vol 58, 1964, 239—51.

[8] In a letter to John Forster, 1 April 1841, relatively late in Colburn's career, one should note. See *The Pilgrim Edition of the Letters of Charles Dickens*, eds. Madeline House, Kathleen Tillotson and Graham Storey (London, 1974), Vol III, p. 599.

[9] *Harriet Martineau's Autobiography*, ed. Maria Weston Chapman (Boston, 1878), Vol I, pp. 400–4.

[10] Edmund Downey, *Charles Lever: His Life in His Letters* (London, 1906), Vol I, p. 132.

[11] Melnyk's close analysis of the imputed and actual malefaction is examined, at length, in Chapter 5 of her doctoral dissertation.

reprint publisher, he is reported to have called on Lady Morgan who, in 1814, had been the first 'name' author in his stable—a £1,000 a novel writer (Colburn always ensured such payments were generally known). He owed much to her, in the creation of his mature (and profitable) publishing style—books with a 'fashionable' lustre to them. He ostensibly wanted her to sign over the copyright for one of her novels: when he left, the near-blind authoress found that he had secretly substituted a form which assigned to him *all* her literary property. A kind of before-burial grave robbing.[12]

Colburn was, among all else, a pirate (not, it should be granted, unusual in the nineteenth century British book trade, and virtually universal in the American). In 1839, he published Jared Sparks's biography of Washington without authorization. Other examples of, principally European, titles could be cited as examples of Colburn's buccaneering ways.[13]

No publisher merited more than Henry Colburn the nickname Byron is supposed to have coined with his much-quoted jibe, 'now Barabbas was a publisher'.[14]

Oddly, Colburn (a publisher the author of *Don Juan* would normally not have touched with a barge pole) purported—on one peculiarly rascally occasion—to have published Byron as the author of England's first vampire tale. It's a pure Colburn episode.[15]

Colburn's opportunism became a byword. In 1843, he had his hack, Frederic Shoberl, assemble a plagiarized mish-mash piece of silver forkery entitled *The Tuft-*

---

[12] Lionel Stevenson, *The Wild Irish Girl* (London, 1936), p. 312.

[13] By way of mitigation, one may note Colburn's support throughout the 1840s and 1850s for an international copyright agreement, detailed on pages 166–167 of Melnyk's dissertation.

[14] In fact, it originated, probably, with Thomas Campbell—a writer with close connections with Colburn (see below).

[15] See below, Chapter 10.

Hunter,[16] published under the name of an aristocratic hack, Lord William Pitt Lennox (who hired himself out for social events as a veteran of Waterloo, the Iron Duke's *aide de campe*, no less). Using bona-fide (sometimes spurious) titled authors in this way was a Colburn specialty. Colburn then demanded that his *New Monthly Magazine* applaud *The Tuft-Hunter*. Thomas Hood, the editor, refused to pervert his review pages and resigned.[17] Colburn was a pioneer of this kind of sales 'stunt' and outrageous gimmickry for the sale of his books—'hype' it is called, nowadays. It could be called Colburnism. He merely did it better than his rivals.

John Blackwood—cut from finer publishing cloth—records with heavy irony in 1843: 'Colburn's last feat in the art of puffing a book (viz. by causing Col. Davidson to have him up in police court for the return of his manuscript, and then publishing the book within three days) has excited the admiration and envy of the whole booktrade'.[18] Such pranks actually stank in the nostrils of a Victorian book trade keen to gentrify itself.

Colburn inspired some of the best book-trade jokes, jests and witticisms of his time. Many are still amusing. The pre-eminently witty Sydney Smith teased the publisher mercilessly, when Colburn called to solicit a novel from him:

> Colburn went and made his proposal, with many expressions of admiration for the rev. gentleman's talent. The Canon thought he would test him, so said he liked the proposal much; that he would have an Archdeacon for a hero, and make him intrigue with the Pew-opener, and that under the Hassock would be

---

[16] Slang for 'snob'.

[17] See J. C. Reid, *Thomas Hood* (London, 1963), p. 20.

[18] Oliphant, Vol I, p. 356. Mrs. Oliphant quotes from John Blackwood, writing in 1843. The book referred to is Colonel C. J. Davidson's *Diary of Travels and Adventures in Upper India*.

a good place for depositing the love letters. 'Oh', says Colburn, 'we will leave all that to your well known taste and judgement!' and came away cock-a-hoop.[19]

Bulwer-Lytton (who had taken a small fortune from Colburn in payments) imagined God going round London with the Bible copyright:

> When He calls at New Burlington Street Colburn does not dispute the general merit of the work but doubts it will take with the fashionable world. He suggests ... a few piquant anecdotes about the court of King Herod.[20]

The *Athenaeum*, not normally a comic paper, devoted the front page of its issue of 1 July 1829, to an extended burlesque of dealings at 'Colophon's' office. Colophon, who specializes in silver fork ('fashionable') fiction is overwhelmed with business which brings him in £10,000 a year. A fabulous sum. One 'noble' authoress corrects her proofs upstairs. Another ['Lady Amelia Aubrey' = Lady Charlotte Bury] has come in to haggle, like a fishwife, about terms for her latest novel of high life. Colophon offers an extra £100 if her ladyship will insert 'the secret history of the elopement with which the papers are now filled'. Manuscript to be supplied by the end of the week, before the scandal cools.

Colburn is immortalized, with contemptuous joviality, in William Maginn's novel, *Whitehall: Or the Days of George IV*, as Harry Badger.[21] He is 'Bungay' to Richard Bentley's 'Bacon' (birds of a shabby feather) in a couple of Thackeray's novels (*Pendennis* and *Philip*). *Pendennis* contains an extensive, and unkind, sub-narrative of the

---

[19] Oliphant, Vol II, pp. 356–357.

[20] Michael Sadleir, *Bulwer and his Wife: A Panorama* (London, 1933), pp. 204–205.

[21] See Melnyk op cit. pp. 86–88.

Yours truly
T. Campbell

THE EDITOR OF THE NEW MONTHLY

fratricidal Bentley-Colburn feud, and caricatures of both publishing hustlers. Colburn lived to read *Pendennis*. There is no surviving evidence that it hurt his feelings. He was, by the late 1840s, immune to barbs.

Some of the satire directed against Colburn was more physical and came closer to sticks and stones than words. It probably did hurt. Cyrus Redding and S. C. Hall have left a hilarious picture of the henpecked Colburn ducking teapots thrown by his virago of a first wife.[22] Virtually nothing else is known of that union, other than that there were no children.[23]

The diminutive Colburn was sneered at for his unprepossessing stature. 'The little man', Thomas Campbell called him.[24] Thomas Hood (formerly Colburn's editor on his flagship magazine, *The New Monthly*) was inspired to doggerel:

> Now a Colburn I knew in his person so small
> That he seemed the half-brother of nothing at all,
> Yet in spirit a Dwarf may be big;
> But his mind was so narrow, his soul was so dim,
> Where's the wonder if all I remember of him
> Is—a suit of Boys' clothes and a wig![25]

A low blow, one might call it.

One of the arguments examined in the following pages is that, unscrupulous as they surely were on occasion, Colburn's business practices were, as regards the use of advertising publicity stunts and opinion formation, merely

---

22 Cyrus Redding, *Yesterday and Today* (London, 1863), Vol III, p. 80. S. C. Hall, *Retrospect of a Long Life* (New York, 1883), p. 182.

23 Rather more is known of the second Mrs. Colburn, who went on, after widowhood, to become Mrs. John Forster; Forster was Dickens's closest friend and biographer. See below, chapter 36.

24 Stevenson, p. 272.

25 Reid, p. 202.

'ahead of their time'—twentieth-century publishing styles in the nineteenth century. But can that outweigh Colburn's professional delinquencies? It's an open question.

In his authoritative catalogue of nineteenth-century fiction, Michael Sadleir, the most distinguished of collectors and bibliophiles, concurs as regards the proto-modernity of his commercial practices but denounces Colburn, in the final analysis, as an opportunistic peddler of shoddy books, a harbinger of the sadly depraved mores of Sadleir's own book trade: 'he was a book manufacturer, not a publisher, and his kind are with us to this day.'[26] Hard words. Colburn inspired few other kinds of word. Some more thoughtful analysis is called for.

---

[26] M. Sadleir, *XIX Century Fiction* (Cambridge, 1951), Vol II p. 113. Sadleir was a senior director of the publishing firm Constable's, a bibliophile and a historical (neo-Victorian romance—famously *Fanny by Gaslight*) novelist. For a summary of his career and achievement see John Sutherland, 'Michael Sadleir and his Collection of Nineteenth-Century Fiction', *Nineteenth-Century Literature* (September, 2001).

THE CASE FOR THE DEFENCE

Despite all the hard things said against him, Colburn can be convincingly argued to have been professionally innovative and a force for constructive change in the rapidly evolving London book trade. Mrs. Oliphant (a Blackwoods author to the core) sneered that Colburn ('Scylla') reduced publishing to a 'system'.[27] She meant it as an insult, but it can be turned on its head as a compliment. More than most, Colburn saw which way the wind was blowing.

As a publisher, Colburn's main claim to posthumous repair of his reputation is his troop of 'name' authors who appeared under his imprint: Lady Morgan, Disraeli, Bulwer-Lytton, Captain Marryat, G.P.R. James, Mrs. Oliphant, Frances Trollope, Anthony Trollope, Richard Cobbold, R. S. Surtees. He published Frances Burney's *Diary and Letters;* William Hazlitt's *Table Talk* and *The Spirit of the Age;* Charles Darwin's *Narrative of the Voyage of H.M.S. Beagle;* and the first British editions of James Fenimore Cooper, Benjamin Franklin, and Washington Irving.

Many authors would not have had a start in the careers they later enjoyed, nor have made it into authorship at all, were it not for Henry Colburn. He launched the careers of Captain Marryat (with *Frank Mildmay,* in 1829), of Disraeli (all of whose early fashionable fiction and the political world-changing 'Young England' trilogy he published), and of

---

27 Oliphant, Vol I, pp. 395, 495.

Bulwer-Lytton. Lady Morgan, Mrs. Gore, Mrs. Trollope (he was, arguably, something of a male feminist)—the bulk of whose fiction he published—are respectable second-rank authors.

While certain authors sought to distance themselves from Colburn and others felt themselves somehow bilked, many were grateful for the opportunities he gave them. Would Anthony Trollope, for example, have persevered with fiction (rather than directing all his effort towards his post-office career) had Colburn not published his second and third works? (He may have hoped to palm them off to the reading public as the work of Anthony's better-known mother, Mrs. Trollope, whom he also published, and was tight-fisted about remuneration with both Trollopes.) There survives a poignant letter from Emily Brontë offering him her first novel. Colburn, for a certainty, would have marketed the author of *Wuthering Heights* with more flair than did T. C. Newby—a publisher of even lower repute. Although often accused of cheating authors, Colburn was a pioneer in paying his top authors four-figure sums. It's not the highest of praise. But he was never tight-fisted with 'quality'.

The insularity of the British reading public is legendary. There are two ways of losing money, British publishing lore instructs: publishing poetry and publishing translations. Colburn (poetry was not one of his long suits, although he would have sold his soul to publish Byron) played a significant role in the opening of British literary culture to continental culture, notably that of France (initially at a period when the countries were at war). He was, for instance, the first publisher of Stendhal in England, although the (habitual) lateness of his payments provoked a frenzy of Gallic denunciation against '*cet animal ... de demi-fripon de Colburn*'. He was, among the major publishers of the day, among a small minority in knowing what *demi-fripon* meant ('tiny rogue').[28] No other publisher of his day

[28] M. Gautier, *Captain Frederick Marryat* (Paris, 1973), p. 100.

did more for translations from the French. One suspects he may have undertaken some himself.

Although Michael Sadleir asserts 'he had no literary taste', there is convincing evidence to the contrary.[29] Colburn kept to the end of his (prosperous) life his finest literary copyrights—including, most remuneratively, that of Pepys's diary. That was not the act of a man without taste. The property descended, via his widow's remarriage to John Forster, Dickens's biographer (the oddest of turns, in a continuously strange life).

What then, as regards the machineries of British publishing, did Colburn do that should raise his reputation and make us see him as a good thing? Even his inveterate critic, Sadleir, granted that Colburn 'revolutionised publishing in its every aspect'. The phrase 'every aspect' is worth thinking about. And one should remember that Sadleir was, inter alia, a twentieth-century publisher of distinction.

What does 'revolution' mean? In the largest sense, Colburn demonstrated, by example and practice, the need for consolidation between hitherto dismembered arms of the London book world. Beginning his career at apprentice level in the London West End circulating-library business, he went on, having learned at the counter what the 'carriage trade' customer wanted, to become the undisputed market leader in the publication of three-volume novels and (sub-Murray) travel books. The three-decker novel, of which Colburn became a leading supplier, went on to become the foundation-stone of the 'Leviathan' library system (Mudie's and Smith's) and created a seventy-year stability in the publishing, distribution and reception of English fiction. Its life lasted, astonishingly, from the 1820s to the 1890s. Colburn, from his earliest days in Conduit and Albemarle streets, developed a face-to-face 'feel' for what would catch the customer's fancy. He had a weather vane sensitivity to the currents of popular taste and demand.

---

[29] See Melnyk, op cit., passim.

THE FRASERIANS

Moreover, he developed formidable skills in stimulating popular taste, the better to feed it with his wares. Time and again in the taunts and insults leveled against him—and in that 'Prince of Puffers' nickname—one finds the complaint that Colburn's use of advertisement to promote and publicize his books is, somehow, against the rules of the game. No gentleman would descend to mere hucksterism. The accusation rings hollow. Colburn was, quite simply, ahead of his time. *Fraser's Magazine*, for instance, noted with scathing sarcasm on 1 April 1830 that Colburn's office had a 'Publicity Department'. Terribly bad form, it is implied. (It is worth noting, in passing, that the literary world of Colburn's day was more politicized than ours. Colburn tended towards the liberal side. *Fraser's* was ferociously Tory.)[30]

Any thoroughgoing defence of Colburn could well begin by locating him not in the history of publishing but in the history of publicity. The scale of Colburn's advertising budget is breathtaking when one converts Victorian currency into modern sterling.[31] At his zenith, in the 1820s, he is supposed to have expended thousands of pounds on pushing his books. According to John Chapman, a contemporary publisher (not to be confused with Chapman and Hall), Colburn and Bentley, in the years of their fraught alliance spent £27,000 advertising their firm's books between 1829 and 1832.[32] If true, it's an extraordinary amount.

Colburn's 'puffing engine', or advertising system, was sophisticated, diverse and imaginative in its operations. The name of an author, or the amount paid them, might be publicized (or ostentatiously withheld, if the author were—or could be supposed to be—noble, notorious, or a

---

[30] See Miriam Thrall, *Rebellious Fraser's: Nol Yorke's Magazine in the Days of Maginn, Carlyle and Thackeray* (New York, 1934).

[31] The most convenient rule of thumb is to multiply Regency sums by fifty.

[32] This figure, which has been frequently cited, originates with John Chapman in *Cheap Books and How to Get Them* (London, 1852), p. 7.

high official). Colburn was rumoured to employ diners-out, who would talk up his books. In his relationship (fraught and short-lived though it was) with Richard Bentley, Colburn proved that fluid quasi-industrial partnership, not congeries (or 'dynastic' houses), was the future of the trade. The fact that he was (almost certainly) illegitimate meant there was never any family or patriarchal 'drag' on his activities. Colburn was a pioneer 'middle-sized', general trade publisher, with a distinct 'house style'. These were to be the cutting edge of British publishing in the late nineteenth- and twentieth-century. In an age of 'agglomerization', and mega-publishers, many would argue they still should be.

In the late 1820s, Colburn and Bentley set up the 'Standard Novel' reprint—its genetic descendant is the hardback-paperback sequence in today's book trade. In 1814, Colburn founded the *New Monthly Magazine*. In 1817, he set up England's first serious weekly review, the *Literary Gazette*. In 1828, he helped found the *Athenaeum*—distant parent of today's *New Statesman*. His behaviour as a magazine proprietor and editor at large was at times outrageous. But the link he forged between higher journalism and literature was momentous. In the great crash of 1826—which swept like a hurricane through the British book trade—Colburn demonstrated that a canny publisher, with his wits about him, could not only survive but thrive. Crisis was, as the Chinese proverb has it, opportunity.

Taking the large view of his long career one notes how his business acumen extended to diversification. He mixed his fiction-based list with memoir, travelogue, literary magazines and books—such as his impressive list of military books—with appeal to specific affiliation groups.

The major impression one takes away from every twist and turn of his tortuous, slippery-as-an-eel career is that Henry Colburn was cleverer than his opposition in the book trade. That quality redeems something, if not everything, in his nefarious career. Or was it so nefarious?

COLBURN'S ORIGINS

Colburn's date of birth is unrecorded—or, at least, it is recorded so variously as to amount to the same thing. This is unusual for someone of standing in the nineteenth century and raises, following the most sensational rumour attaching to his rumour-encrusted career (see above), that he was an illegitimate child of some high, even royal, dignitary, launched in business with money from his father.[33] It is possible Colburn put into circulation mendacious pedigrees for himself as he routinely did with dubiously aristocratic purveyors of his silver-forkery. But if true, this bar-sinister, blue-blooded paternity would explain, in addition to the elusive birthdate, such peculiarities as his appearing to have a sizeable capital at the very beginning of his publishing career; his extravagant adulation of royalty and nobility (Colburn was the publisher of Burke's various works on the British peerage, from 1826 onwards—a labour of love, one assumes; his list is never without its shabby purple fringe of raddled 'Countesses', 'Ladies', and 'Duchesses'); and his obsession with mysterious authors

---

[33] The probable rumour that Colburn had royal parentage, specifically the Duke of York (see above) comes from S. M. Ellis, *William Harrison Ainsworth and his Friends* (London, 1911). Ellis cites William Hazlitt as originating the story. It is S. C. Hall, in *Retrospect*, p. 182, who records the rumour that Colburn was the illegitimate offspring of Lord Landsdowne.

whose true, high-born identity must be kept secret. Like his own.

Most significantly, this version of Colburn's birth (or something like it—other unidentified 'respectable' parentage, for example) would overthrow one of the recurrent insults hurled against him in his lifetime—'guttersnipe'.

This insult is contradicted by the observable evidence to the contrary. Those who have examined his literary remains are left in no doubt that Colburn was well educated. On this front—personal cultivation—Henry Colburn could hold his own with any of the most distinguished in the trade. His English was excellent (the spelling is usually perfect in even his most hurried notes); he was fluent in both written and spoken French; his polished manners put him at ease with both his titled authors and his well-heeled clientele; and, judging by his intimate knowledge of Paris, he had enjoyed at least one extended stay there. Despite the lack of hard evidence, it is a lot easier to accept Colburn's ties to the aristocracy than the near-miracle that would otherwise be necessary to explain all of these advantages in a working- or even middle-class lad. Let alone a 'guttersnipe'.

COLBURN'S AGE AND BIRTH: A PUZZLE WITH SOME IMPORTANCE

The most detailed and thoughtful speculation on Colburn's mysterious origin is that of Michael Sadleir, who wrote it as part of his unfinished monograph on Richard Bentley. Sadleir takes on board the usual Colburnian themes but moulds them into an original theory that merits quotation in its entirety (a man of letters and publisher, born in 1888, Sadleir may, conceivably, have picked up some gossip that fed into his suspiciously elaborate 'guess'):

> My guess is that he was the illegitimate son of an Englishman by a French mother, that his name was fictitious, and that he grew up in France. This is admittedly pure conjecture. But the mystery of Colburn's origin is so marked that there must have been something to hide. His French affiliations, his familiarity with the French language and his knowledge of Paris indicate that he lived in France for some years, and these can only have been the years of boyhood and adolescence, for once in evidence in London he remained there. If he were a love-child, he would naturally have been cared for by his mother or her relatives, and, assuming that he was born early in the 1780s and came to England in his late 'teens, the change of residence may well have been connected with

an émigré flight from the Revolution. This suggests on his mother's side an aristocratic or at any rate an anti-Jacobin origin—a theory supported by his later activity in publishing Bonapartist literature. It may be added that the suddenness with which he set up as a publisher implies that funds were available, and these would most likely have been supplied by an English father of rank or of substance. When exactly he came to London is not known, but he seems to have established himself there in the publishing and lending library business during the early eighteen hundreds.[34]

Though Sadleir grants it is 'pure conjecture', his theory manages to knit together seamlessly all the known facts without resorting to wholly improbable explanations. Unless someone turns up evidence to the contrary, Sadleir's version of Colburn's personal history is, it is safe to conclude, the leading contender to be the accepted version.[35]

The only flaw, of course, is that Sadleir casually assumes that Colburn 'was born early in the 1780s'. No reason for this date is offered. But some published sources offer a handful of clues that may well support Sadleir's guess. In its notice of Colburn's death in 1855, *The Illustrated London News* wondered, at the time of his passing, whether 'he had not exceeded the Scriptural period of threescore and ten'.[36] This, of course, may simply have been a deduction from facial appearance: there are, sadly, few portraits of him at any period of his life.

S. C. Hall recalled that Colburn was 'somewhat aged' at the time of his 1830 marriage,[37] which could describe

---

[34] Sadleir Papers, 360, 1–12.

[35] The main account of Colburn's life, in his own day, is his obituary notice in the *Gentleman's Magazine,* November 1855.

[36] *Illustrated London News,* Aug. 1855, 231.

[37] Hall, op cit. 1, 316.

a man of forty-five or fifty years, but the phrasing is too imprecise to be of much value. Perhaps the best clue is simply the duration of Colburn's public life: it spanned nearly fifty years from his death back to his publishing debut in 1806, at which time one would expect him to have been at least twenty years old if not older. Such calculations add support to the shrewd Sadleirian guess that he was born in the 'early 1780s'.

This date, however, is contradicted by the lone primary source that notes, with any precision, Colburn's age: the record of his burial. This simple ledger entry, evidently made at his interment on 23 August 1855, lists his age at the time of his death as being sixty-five.[38] This is somewhat difficult to accept. Again working backwards from his death, we find that Colburn would have been merely sixteen years of age when he published his first batch of books (nine volumes of them) in 1806. Knowing that he served an apprenticeship before that, we would have to believe that he entered the commercial library trade at the age of ten or perhaps twelve—highly unlikely if not completely inconceivable. Could a teenager have commissioned these books, paid for their production—even proofread them?

Richard Bentley was granted an intimate knowledge of his former partner and included some of it in his unpublished obituary of Colburn, where he tackles the age issue head on. Bentley records, in his private reminiscences about Colburn, that the former publisher died 'in, I believe, his 71st year, although the coffin-plate [...] described him as aged 65'. Therefore, the age on the coffin plate corresponds with that in the burial register, but probably not that of the coffin's contents.

Colburn's being seventy-one at the time of his death makes much greater sense. It means that he was twenty-two at the time of his first publications—still young but not unreasonably so—and squares with Sadleir's guess as well

---

[38] Bishops' Transcripts [of Burials], entry 24557.

as all of the other circumstantial evidence. It also has the advantage of coming from someone who knew Colburn intimately for more than a decade. For all of these reasons, we have accepted this age and accordingly used 1784 as the year of his birth throughout this book.

Nonetheless we, and the reader, may wonder at the pretence of being sixty-five years old in 1855. It is possible that someone made an honest mistake: his grieving widow or the emissary she sent to make the burial arrangements, for example. It is more likely, however, that this was a deliberate ploy to continue—or, indeed, set the seal on— the long campaign of obfuscation carried out by Colburn all his life. Always economical with the truth, he lied himself into the grave: his final stunt, some would sneer. Friendlier verdicts are possible.

According to the scanty sources on his life which we have, Colburn began his book-trade career while still a 'lad', as assistant to William Earle, bookseller and librarian, at 47 Albemarle Street. Richard Bentley confirmed this fact when he noted in a throwaway remark in his diary on 25 August 1859 that he had, that day, met up with 'Mr. Earle, son of the bookseller Earle of Albemarle Street, to whom Colburn was bound apprentice'.

Earle's establishment, in the epicentre of London's fashionable West End, is described as a 'fashionable lounging place' and evidently helped form young Henry's sense of what a clientele for books was and how it could be best exploited. Two large trends had served to expand the nineteenth-century market for books: one was the increased spending power and leisure of the upper (competently literate) classes, of both sexes—Colburn was always attentive to the female reader. The other large trend was the increasing literacy and political consciousness of the lower classes (the highpoint of which was the 1832 Reform Act). For Colburn, the second of these trends was nugatory. His indifference to the 'hidden public', the self-improving reader, hungry for cheap reading matter, was total. He was never a 'popular educator', such as Charles Knight (one of Colburn's most appalled critics).

It is worth noting, however, that Colburn likely had a greater *middle-class* audience than has previously been acknowledged. Though it has often been remarked that his silver-fork novels in particular read like training manuals for those aspiring to join the *ton*, their appeal was not limited to this tiny faction. Cheryl Wilson demonstrates that the middle class as a whole enjoyed increasing leisure time in which to read and more disposable income with which to purchase books or join libraries: 'The period saw the cultural and economic transformation of novels from luxury items to staples of the middle-class home'.[39] The most cleverly constructed silver-fork novels were 'able to maintain their appeal to multiple audiences, making promises about social mobility to middle-class readers while assuring fashionable readers of their protected and insular position'.[40] This was clearly the shrewdest approach in an industry where novels were still not cheap.

Of Colburn's 996 books listed in the *English Catalogue*, only 310 cost less than £1.[41] This was more than the English national wage. Colburn was never a dogmatic and certainly never a 'political' producer of reading material. Self-preservation, and the risks involved in 'dangerous'

---

[39] Cheryl A. Wilson, *Fashioning the Silver Fork Novel* (London: Pickering & Chatto, 2012) 127.

[40] Ibid., 141.

[41] The compendium volumes of *The English Catalogue of Books, 1801—1836* (London, 1914) and *The English Catalogue, 1835—1862* (London 1864) have been used in creating a general outline of Colburn's book production. This source has known weaknesses; it often overlooks new, or cheaper, editions and misses many works altogether. But it does supply a large enough sample for a general picture of Colburn's activities in his forty-seven years of trading. Many of his office records, and file copies, lodged with his successor Hutchinson's, were destroyed in the World War Two Blitz.

books, doubtless played a part. The young Colburn must have registered the spectacle of fellow-publishers like Richard Carlisle going to jail for putting out 6d editions of Paine's *Rights of Man*. For the whole of his publishing life Colburn stuck, cautiously, to the carriage trade which he knew. Though a cautious approach, it proved a wise one: carving out his own fashionable niche left Colburn free of direct competitors.

His politics were generally Liberal but he eschewed radicalism entirely. He was, nonetheless, happy to suppress partisan feeling and publish a Conservative author like Disraeli (notably his highly political 'Young England' trilogy). When, that is, it paid. The reasons that Disraeli chose to be published by a publisher he calumniated as a 'bawd' are discussed below.

Returning to what little we know of Colburn's early career, the word 'apprenticeship', with reference to his years with Earle, raises a host of questions: Who decided that Colburn was to go into publishing? Who was the responsible adult that 'bound' Colburn to Earle by paid indenture? The five years' instruction would not have been cheap. Did Earle know about Colburn's origins? Was he a friend or acquaintance of Colburn's family?

The answers to these questions remain frustratingly elusive and, in fact, we cannot even settle the simple question of which years, precisely, Colburn worked for Earle. The year 1800 as the starting point seems a strong possibility, considering that sixteen was a usual age for apprenticeship during this period (it was the age at which Bentley himself began his printing apprenticeship[42]), although fourteen would not have been impossible.

In the same 1859 diary entry quoted above, Richard Bentley remarked that: 'it is said Colburn behaved badly to Mr. Earle's sister'. This vague allegation ('said'? by whom?) sits uneasily with Bentley's later remark in his

---

[42] Sadleir, op cit. 360, 7.

diary that: 'whatever faults Colburn might have had he was a gentleman as regards ladies' (31 July 1860). It is, of course, possible that his younger self did not yet possess that gentlemanly virtue. Whether Colburn's implied misbehaviour with Miss Earle was a factor in his leaving her brother's Albemarle Street establishment is now beyond knowing, but it is recorded that by 1806 he was established at Morgan's Public Library at 48-50 Conduit Street, also in the high Mayfair district of London.

Colburn's junior and senior management of the library was to last until 1820, but details of Morgan's concern are not plentiful. It seems to have been much like any other fashionable circulating library—a place to meet others of similar social standing, with social amenities (arm chairs, for example), while choosing volumes of the day too expensive for the reader to purchase outright. But it is clear the ambitious young Colburn wanted his establishment, when he came to have one, to be better than those of his West End rivals. He assured the public, in an advertisement in one of his 1808 publications, that his library

> Now stands *unrivalled*, embracing a most general Selection of Works in every Branch of English, French and Italian Literature; to which are regularly added all new English and Foreign Works; including Magazines, Reviews, Pamphlets, &c. and immediately on their Publication or arrival in Town.

It was not only his 'town' subscribers he catered for. Colburn set his sights beyond London and promised in other advertisements to post books to subscribers anywhere in the country. This by horse-drawn coach.

An advertisement in the *Literary Gazette* (a Colburn-owned journal at the time) for 8 November 1817 gives a good overview of the establishment of his library's business in its peak years. 'Mr. Colburn', the advertisement boasted, offers 'upwards of FIFTY THOUSAND VOLUMES' ('upwards' is the true Colburn touch). The library's 'Terms of Subscription' were complicated, to the point of specifying the size of books (quarto, octavo, etc.) members might borrow and the different terms applying to town and country members. Class 1 subscribers paid five guineas, Class 2 four guineas, and Class 3 paid a guinea and a half—all per annum for variable privileges. Colburn declared himself confident that all of his subscribers would benefit from 'the various new arrangements he has lately concluded in London, and his Continental connexions'.[43]

'Continental' meant, primarily, 'French'. And overwhelmingly high-toned. Colburn, catalogues confirm, published French works in their original language and in English translations from the very beginning of his career. Many of these were memoirs—often by aristocratic French *émigrés* fleeing the aftermath of the Revolution and the Wars—but a substantial number were novels in translation or their original form. Colburn published works by such worthies as the Marchioness de Sillery (Madame de Genlis), the Comtesse de Lichtenau, the Baroness de Staël-Holstein, and the Vicomte de Chateaubriand. These books often bore the imprint '*A Paris et se trouve à Londres, chez Colburn, Libraire*', or something similar. We can only guess at the business details which lay behind them.

Colburn might simply have had a reciprocal agreement with a Paris firm, wherein each published certain works and distributed them along with the other's publications in their own country. Colburn might even, conceivably, have had a branch office in Paris, although one would have expected to find some surviving documentation of such a venture. Some works may have been simply pirated in the expectation that authors might later claim payment.

Whatever the precise nature of his ties across the channel, they were important enough to draw Colburn and his then printer, Richard Bentley, to Paris in 1821 (for which see

---

[43] Pg. 304.

below) and to prompt Lady Caroline Lamb to write: 'I am going to Paris can I do anything for you' to her publisher-cum-librarian.[44]

All this, of course, leads us back to the speculation about Colburn's natal origins being, as Sadleir supposes, in France and confirms that his 'connexions' there were every bit as good as his advertisements implied.

---

[44] National Art Library, F.48.E.22, 53–54.

THE RISE OF HENRY COLBURN

Traditional accounts record that Colburn began his career (i.e., he was now out of his apprenticeship) as an 'assistant' to Mr. Morgan but do not record that businessman's first name or the connection (personal or professional) which brought the youthful Colburn into his employ. We might wonder at the young man's transition from bookselling to librarianship, but since the lines between these practices—and publishing—were still fluid during this period, it was not a remarkable move. Literary men, like Thomas Campbell and Thomas Carlyle, used the blanket term 'bookseller' to describe publishers, retailers, and librarians.

The genuinely remarkable thing was Colburn's publishing three books from Morgan's 50 Conduit Street establishment in 1806, apparently mere months after his arrival in the premises. The title pages declare, uncompromisingly, that Colburn is sole proprietor of 'The British and Foreign Library, 50 Conduit Street and New Bond Street'.

Ambidextrously a publisher and circulating library proprietor, Colburn would have his headquarters at Conduit Street until disposing of it to Saunders and Otley in 1824–25, by then having moved to New Burlington Street. London's West End was his natural habitat. He was as at home in it as a fish in water.

Colburn's library activities had an intimate linkage with his practices as a publisher. The flow of volumes across his counter gave him a 'feel' for what the customer wanted—

he had his finger, so to speak, on the reading public's pulse.

There is a primal interest in Colburn's first batch of books under his name, all clearly designed for the circulating library: a four-volume set of Kotzebue's *Tales* (4 vols, 21s), Kotzebue's *Anecdotes* (3 vols, 18s) and a Gothic tale, *The Convent of Notre Dame* (2 vols 9s).[45] The publication in multi-volume form (a hallmark of Colburn's publishing style) is another hangover from his library business: fractionalizing a popular book in this way, involving plentiful white space (innovation in the paper industry had lowered the price of the product), large font, colourful binding (normally undertaken by the library), and generous leading between lines bulked the volumes, and made them readable (the short English day, candlelight, and scarce availability of spectacles was a problem until gaslight, in the mid-century). Above all, it meant three or four customers could be catered for with one title.

The French flavour of Colburn's inaugural nine volumes is pronounced. The following year, 1807, yields seven titles under the Colburn imprint and evidence of his early connection with the polyglot Frederic Shoberl, who translated C. Meiners' *History of the Female Sex*.[46] Its

---

[45] It may be noted, in passing, how expensive these books were for the private purchaser, a factor which helped form the library, collective use, system that became a major feature of the 19th-century book trade.

[46] A multi-lingual man of letters, Shoberl was not a member of Colburn's staff but what would now be called a freelancer. Having translated and prepared a number of works for the publisher from his earliest years in the publishing business (and probably more than are documented), he was later associated with Colburn's *New Monthly Magazine*. There is recurrent confusion of Frederic with his son William, who also worked for Colburn, albeit a few decades later. A general rule of thumb is that the Colburn and Bentley partnership divides Frederic Shoberl's era from William's. An additional problem is that some sources misread Shoberl as Schubert, which can probably be ascribed to illegible handwriting and the rarity of the name.

four volumes were originally published in German, in 1800. The contents are indicated by its laborious, but teasing, subtitle: '*Comprising a View of the Habits, Manners, and Influence of Women, Among all Nations, from the Earliest Ages to the Present Time.*' The word 'Sex' probably enhanced interest. Colburn was always alive to such hints of daring things between his covers.

According to the *English Catalogue* (patchy, but the best bibliometric source we have)[47], 1808 was a year of consolidation, with no new titles listed, but a creditable and growing backlist. His library experience gave him sensitivity as to how long a book's 'day' would last, and how long it should be kept in stock, or on the shelf, or in the warehouse.

In 1809, Colburn spurted ahead with twelve works listed in the *English Catalogue:* eight fiction, three memoirs, one travel book. This would be the main tripod on which his subsequent book-publishing output was to rest. He rarely experimented beyond it.[48]

Of Colburn's 1809 titles, no fewer than eight are translations from the French. Between 1806 and 1815— that is, between the battles of Trafalgar and Waterloo— Colburn published 108 works of which 53 are of French origin or on French topics. To the end of his publishing career, he had an interest in such books. And, clearly, there was a market. It seems likely that Colburn was active in what is now called co-publishing: putting out a work simultaneously in French and English for a few shillings extra to cover the translation.

---

[47] New online resources promise, when complete, more reliable and comprehensive source-material: see http://www.british-fiction.cf.ac.uk/index.html and http://www.victorianresearch.org/atcl/.

[48] Matthew Rosa, in *The Silver Fork School* (New York, 1936) claims that at the start of his career Colburn published 'pietistic works'. They have not been identified and were, presumably, not published with his name on them.

S. Morgan

AUTHOR OF "O'DONNEL".

Colburn may have been attracted to foreign—specifically French—authors by the ease with which they could be pirated or underpaid. But it is also likely that there was an *émigré* population around Conduit Street who patronized the appropriately named British and Foreign Library. Nor would the well-heeled British subscriber, cooped up in England by the Napoleonic Wars, be averse to *touristique* books. At this early stage, Colburn evidently fixed on the main elements in his lifelong publishing formula: books of travel (preferably by titled travellers) and escapist fiction (preferably by titled authors) that transported the middle-class reader into the salons and foreign resorts of the high born.

Throughout Colburn's working life, voyage and travelogue literature occupied about an eighth of his output (since these books stayed in print a long time, they were more of a selling presence in his backlist than the fraction suggests). And although he never rivaled Murray (who did, where travel literature was concerned?) Colburn has to his credit such premier titles as Eliot Warburton's *The Crescent and the Cross* (a work he was proud of publishing, since he kept the copyright on winding up his firm in 1853), various works by James Silk Buckingham, and—the jewel in his crown—Charles Darwin's *Journal* of the Beagle voyage (1839). That, alone, is a title which goes a long way to redeeming Colburn's reputation.

In the years up to 1817, Colburn established his career-long hallmark preference for aristocratic authoresses with handles—prominent on the title page—to their names. He never saw a tiara, or a haughty flashing eye, that he did not like to see in print. No publisher 'truckled' more than Henry Colburn. There are, in his first decade, multiple works by Madame de Genlis (ten titles between 1806 –1817) and Madame de Stael (seven works). These were his top-bill women authors until Lady Morgan came on the scene, and together with Madame Sophie Cottin (whose complete works in fourteen volumes Colburn published in

1811), they point the way to Colburn's later stock-in-trade, the English 'silver fork' novel.

He had other strings to his bow. In 1812, he published *The Milesian Chief* (4 vols., 12s) by the new Irish writer, Charles Maturin. The novel, which cost Colburn only a speculative £80, outright purchase, was popular and influential. It is plausibly supposed to have inspired Scott's *The Bride of Lammermoor*, as well as a genre of picaresque Irish, military, fiction that was later popularized by another Colburn author, Charles Lever. Colburn would go on to have a regular line of Irish books (it opened his connection with Anthony Trollope). He may have had an agency in Dublin, one of the centres of the British book trade in the early nineteenth century.

Otherwise 1812, as regards publication, was a fairly still time for Colburn, with only eleven titles, of which six are French in origin. But a reason for the quietus can be suggested.

THE 1812 BREAK INTO INDEPENDENCE

We can explain Colburn's being able to publish so much, so early, if we accept the hypothesis that it was his unidentified but wealthy relatives who invested the necessary capital to set him up in the book trade. What is harder to explain is the nature of the arrangement with Morgan that allowed Colburn to publish from his premises without including the senior partner's name on any of the title pages of his early books.

Morgan was never connected, in title-page print at least, with Colburn's publishing interests and he drops entirely from view in 1812. Even the library which earlier carried the single surname 'Morgan' is no longer formally referred to as being his. From this point on, Colburn's title pages refer to the Conduit Street business as the 'English and Foreign Circulating Library'; the 'English, French, and Italian Subscription Library'; the 'British and Foreign Public Library'; and any number of variations on these themes. The advertisements for Colburn's publications cut through the niceties and refer to their origin as the 'Public Library' or, most tellingly, 'Colburn's Library'. Does this mean that Colburn bought the Morgan establishment lock, stock, and barrel in 1806? Possibly. But a twenty-two-year-old single-handedly running a joint lending, bookselling, and publishing venture is a little improbable. It is more likely that Colburn's financial leverage—his capital—allowed him to become the public face of the business, while Morgan quietly managed the place and taught his ambitious, intelligent and well-heeled *protégé* the ropes. Indeed, there is a good case for arguing that Colburn did not become sole proprietor of the library—a truly independent operator—until 1812.

The clinching piece of evidence is to be found not from examining the beginning of Colburn's career but its conclusion. He sold his business upon his retirement in 1853 to the newly-formed partnership of Hurst and Blackett, Daniel Hurst having worked for Colburn for several years previously. The pair began publishing that year, 1853, with the proclamation: 'Successors to Henry Colburn' prominent on their title pages, drawing on the capital of goodwill their venerable predecessor had built up.

After trading on that filial connection as long as was seemly, Hurst and Blackett invented a fresh epithet to give their business the aura of a long-established firm: 'Publishers since 1812'. Since this could not possibly refer to the inception of the house of Hurst and Blackett, it could only refer to the founding of their predecessor Henry Colburn's business. Hurst would have chosen the date based on his long personal acquaintance with Colburn and his access to many of his old business documents—the records destroyed in the 1940s Blitz on London. There is, therefore, substantial justification for accepting the supposition that 1812 was indeed the year that Colburn struck out on his own as a bookman.

FULLY FLEDGED

Now independent, 1813 was a busy year for Henry Colburn: 26 titles, eleven French, five Italian in origin. A small boom was set off by the end (as it was wrongly believed) of the Napoleonic Wars. Europe was no longer an enemy. The following year, 1814, seems to have been make-or-break for Colburn. The main constituent in his dozen-title list is typical of the miscellaneous potboilers which largely comprise his product before 1825, with one notable exception: Lady Morgan's *O'Donnell*. The publication of this three-volume 'national tale' marks the start of a relationship which was to be formative for Colburn. He gave £550 for the copyright—probably the most money he had hitherto laid out for a single title. And Morgan's book did well for him, quickly selling 2,000 copies.[49]

O'Donnell led to the volume which spectacularly lifted the first decade of Colburn's career: Lady Morgan's *France* (1817). The one-word title has the Colburn teasing hook to it. 'Lady' Morgan herself embodied all the ingredients that flattered Colburn's taste as a publisher. She was a glamorous, cosmopolitan, somewhat notorious, titled woman of the world, with Liberal politics, who could turn out fashionable fiction, high-flown memoir, and books of travel as fast as he could print them. Colburn's other top-selling title of 1816–17 was Lady Caroline Lamb's

---

[49] Stevenson, p. 277.

EhBulwer   Alfred Crowquill delt.

AUTHOR OF"THE SIAMESE TWINS".

sensational and scandalous novel—archetype of the silver-fork genre—*Glenarvon;* more of which later.

As was to be his subsequent practice with top-billing, top-selling authors, Colburn bombarded Lady Morgan and Lady Caroline Lamb with large sums of money. He gave Morgan £1,000 for *France,* which promptly went through four editions in England and America and two in France itself; £1,200 for *Florence McCarthy* (1818; five quick-fire editions); and a magnificent £2,000 for *Italy* (1821). Though not a star in the Disraeli or Bulwer-Lytton class, Morgan nevertheless had longevity and would be a solid performer for Colburn for decades.

Alaric A. Watts

THE EDITOR OF "THE LITERARY SOUVENIR".

MAGAZINERY

The other auspicious event of 1814 for Colburn was the founding, on the first of February, of his *New Monthly Magazine and Universal Register.*[50] Initially the venture was set up in opposition to Sir Richard Phillips's radical *Monthly* (Phillips had been Lady Morgan's first publisher, which may have whetted Colburn's rivalry). Colburn soon changed, and recharacterized the title as the *New Monthly Magazine and Literary Journal,* dropping the dull-sounding 'Register'. There were bigger changes. Alaric Watts, one of the *New Monthly's* editors, plausibly claimed Colburn's magazine as the 'seed of that mighty revolution which [has] since sprung up in magazine literature'.[51] It's a grand claim which nonetheless holds up.

One aspect of the 'revolution' Watts talks about was that the journal allowed Colburn to keep 'warm'—and available for his publishing ventures—a stable of 'his' writers. *The New Monthly* could boast, under its string of editors, as distinguished a crew of contributors as any house in London: Bulwer, Disraeli, Gore, Hazlitt, Theodore Hook, Leigh Hunt, Mary Shelley, Sir Charles and Lady Sydney Morgan, Mary Russell Mitford, and Stendhal. Crucially,

---

[50] *The New Monthly* has been the subject of two Ph.D. theses: Grill's, covering 1814 to 1820, and Jones's, covering 1821 to 1830. See the Bibliography for further details.

[51] Oliphant, op cit. I, 498.

Yours faithfully,
Theodore E. Hook

AUTHOR OF "SAYINGS. AND DOINGS"

all of them had published or would go on to publish books under Colburn's imprint. The big name lustre of these writers (brighter in their day than ours, alas) should not detract from the driving force behind the journal—Henry Colburn. Colburn has rarely, if ever, received due credit for bringing such talents together and dexterously presenting them to the public. This is all the more regrettable since the *New Monthly* was one of Colburn's dearest concerns, as the first magazine that he founded, and the recipient of much of his time and energy at a period of life when those energies were at their most vigorous. The *New Monthly* is also, for those who care to look, the magazine that reveals the most about Colburn's reading of current events of public interest, managerial skills, and editorial practice. There were, over the first six years, half a dozen names on the magazine's front page (Frederick Shoberl, John 'Dictionary' Watkins, Alaric Watts, Cyrus Redding, and Thomas Noon Talfourd), but the invisible hand directing the operation was Henry Colburn's.

In form, content and general outreach (through library, family and, particularly, club subscription) the *New Monthly Magazine* looks forward, ultimately, to *Cornhill* and the popular monthly miscellanies of the later century. From 1814 to 1820, the periodical was edited ('conducted') successively by Frederic Shoberl, Dr. John Watkins, and Frederick Watts as *The New Monthly Magazine and Universal Register*. Watts left in 1820, incensed by Colburn's passing-off of Polidori's The Vampyre as Byron's composition.[52]

Sensing the enterprise lacked 'sparkle', a favourite consideration with him, Colburn in January 1821 recruited the veteran literary lion Thomas Campbell to be a figurehead editor. His initial three-year contract also required him to contribute twelve articles per annum for a

---

[52] A general introduction to the *New Monthly*, and Colburn's role in it, will be found in David Higgins, article ('The *New Monthly Magazine*'), The Literary Encyclopedia 22 (Online, October 2006).

Yours &c. Leigh Hunt.

AUTHOR OF "BYRON & HIS CONTEMPORARIES."

salary of £500[53]. Campbell, though unread today, enjoyed
considerable recognition and respect in his own time (he
was, among much else, a founder of London University)
and so was, by Colburn's standard, a good choice. By
professional standards more demanding than Colburn's,
however, he was abysmal: desperately disorganized,
indecisive, unambitious to the point of indolence, timid
about expressing criticism, and oversensitive in reacting
to it. Cyrus Redding, who picked up most of the slack as
the *New Monthly's* sub-editor (he would hack away, behind
the scenes, from 1821 to 1830), illustrated the nature and
extent of Campbell's inadequacy when he remarked, 'I do
not believe the poet ever read through a single number
of the magazine during the whole ten years he was its
editor'.[54] S. C. Hall delivered the same verdict, with a sour
afterthought: 'in short, though a great man, [Campbell]
was utterly unfit to be an editor. I have nearly the same to
say of Theodore Hook, Lytton Bulwer, and Tom Hood,
who were his successors in the editorial chair'.[55]

At the end of Campbell's three-year stint, Colburn
toyed with the idea of replacing him with Horace Smith,
a universally liked man of letters with all the talent of the
incumbent editor but none of the laziness.[56] Unfortunately
for Smith, he lacked Campbell's illustriousness—something
that was proving to be quite as valuable to the *New Monthly*
as Colburn had always thought it would be. He felt justified
in keeping his indolent helmsman on for a further seven
years.

The 'newness' Colburn added to the *New Monthly*—
specifically its injection of 'literariness' and the presence
of literary notables—served to double the magazine's
circulation to around 5,000 copies, most going to libraries

[53] Beattie II, 357.
[54] *Literary Reminiscences* I, 202.
[55] Hall, op cit., I, 314.
[56] Rollins 361.

W. H. Ainsworth —

AUTHOR OF "ROOKWOOD".

and clubs, at a per-issue cost of 3s6d (expensive by the standards of the day—most monthlies and quarterlies charged 1s, like *Blackwoods*, or half a crown, like the *Quarterly*). After Campbell followed the recurrent path of indignant resignation, the magazine (becoming ever more literary in tone) featured a string of editorial eminences: Bulwer-Lytton (who from 1831–33 combined both figurehead and working roles), S. C. Hall (1833–36), Theodore Hook (1837–41), Thomas Hood (1841–43) and finally Harrison Ainsworth, who went on to buy the magazine in 1845. One of Ainsworth's first acts was to follow Colburn in rejecting an early draft of Thackeray's *Vanity Fair* when it was still titled 'Pencil Sketches of English Society', triggering what was to be one of the livelier literary feuds of the decade.[57] The great Vanityfairian never forgave either Ainsworth or Colburn and paid them out with more savage satire than history suggests their offence warranted. Thackeray was good at bearing grudges. Mrs. Gore and Bulwer-Lytton were other targets of his satire of anything associated with Colburn.

In 1820, Colburn had begun the practice of sky-high, 'splash' payments for editors and select contributors. The sums were judiciously leaked to boost the appeal of the paper. It was universally 'known', for example (by carefully disseminated gossip), that Campbell had £500 p.a. for little more than the use of his name, hanging, like a shingle, on the front of the *New Monthly*. As Mary Shelley (a Colburn author) wrote to Leigh Hunt (another Colburn author) in August 1823: 'Do you know that [Horace] Smith gets £200 per ann. from Colburn, clear, regularly, for writing "al suo aggio"—sometimes yes, at times no—for the New Monthly?'[58] The magazine also served as a centre for

---

[57] S. M. Ellis, *William Harrison Ainsworth and his Friends* (London, 1911), II, 250.

[58] *The Letters of Mary Wollstonecraft Shelley*, ed. Betty T. Bennett (Baltimore, 1980), Vol I, p. 374.

Alfred Croquis delt

I D'Israeli

AUTHOR OF "LIFE & CHARACTER OF CHARLES I."

literary dinners, which sucked authors into Colburn's net.

Bulwer was Campbell's closest successor in the editorial chair; not just chronologically (he was contracted on 4 October 1831), but also in terms of furthering the *New Monthly's* reputation as, primarily, an opinion-forming literary periodical. Bulwer had already published bestselling novels with Colburn and had an impressive number of friends who were capable and known writers. Under Bulwer's direction, the *New Monthly* ran pieces by the young John Forster (the future husband of Colburn's widow), Lady Marguerite Blessington, and both Isaac D'Israeli and Benjamin Disraeli. Bulwer was a serving MP at this time and his heavy parliamentary workload, along with his obvious pro-Reform editorial agenda, brought his editorship to an end. In his twenty-two months running the journal, he worried his publisher that he was returning the *New Monthly* to the more political, less literary character it had in its early days. Bulwer-Lytton lost the magazine an estimated one thousand subscribers.[59] Nonetheless it was he who conducted the magazine through the fraught days of the great Bill.

After Bulwer left the post in 1833, Colburn, in some relief, one imagines, installed S. C. Hall, a literary man through and through, as editor. Hall went on to commission (and write) diverting and innocuous articles. Colburn's relief cost him, however. Losing Bulwer-Lytton—a public man rising ever higher—meant losing his aura of extra-literary celebrity as well as the high-quality contributions by him and his circle. This can be seen as marking an inexorable decline for the *New Monthly*, as it slowly reverted to the bland, unremarkable status it had held in 1814. Colburn engineered another relaunch in 1837, this time to join the trend towards humorous magazines and to compete with *Bentley's Miscellany* in particular. Subsequent editors of the rechristened *New Monthly Magazine and Humourist* were,

---

[59] Cyrus Redding, *Literary Reminiscences of Thomas Campbell*, I, 317.

Alfred Croquis del.[?]

AUTHOR OF "VIVIAN GREY."

fittingly, well-known humourists—both of whose best years were behind them: Theodore Hook and Thomas Hood.

Hook, who had published with Colburn back in the distant 1820s, took on the editorship from 1836 until his death in August 1841. A moribund editor for a moribund journal. Thomas Hood picked up where he left off and remained at the post until handing in his resignation in October 1843, ostensibly in protest at Colburn's arrant puffery. Colburn thereafter split the editorial duties with his usual conspirators, such as P. G. Patmore, until selling the *New Monthly* to William Harrison Ainsworth in June 1845. The magazine limped along till its ultimate demise in 1884, its seventieth year.

COLBURN'S BUSINESS PRACTICES EXAMINED

The history of the *New Monthly* yields a wealth of indirect information about its proprietor and his ways. Most prominently, it displays Colburn's fixation with famous names—a fixation clearly shared by a good proportion of the periodical-buying public. 'Articles by Eminent Hands', Thackeray once called them contemptuously. The pages of the *New Monthly* also reveal Colburn's sure grasp of topicality and subjects 'of the day'. Less obviously, one can deduce from Colburn's conduct of the magazine his ability to manage subordinates (and equals), his financial generosity (when necessary), and his insistence on absolute control of anything with his name on it.

One can also deduce that Colburn's relationships with the magazine's writers and editors were conducted with tactful and personal attention. These qualities were clearly employed to good effect in Colburn's handling of the notoriously prickly Thomas Campbell. He was constantly concerned that Colburn's puffery would reflect badly on his own reputation and kicked up regular fusses. Nonetheless, Colburn contrived to stay on good terms with him, not just placating his difficult editor but persuading him that he was valued and liked (the £500 p.a. doubtless helped). At one point, he demanded a sub-editor to assist him and, having received the services of Edward Dubois, impetuously ousted him after working together on only one issue.[60] Colburn replaced the unlucky Dubois without demur and made a point of taking Campbell into his confidence by asking his opinion, for example, about whether he should take on a partner.[61] In all the years of their service together, he seems never to have taken Campbell to task for his dilatory editorial performance. No outbursts of temper are recorded, but vexation must have been felt.

Campbell's letters to Colburn bear witness to the way his employer customarily did business with his employees. In one surviving letter, Campbell explicitly acknowledges Colburn's calm and soothingly diplomatic manner during a disagreement between them:

> I agree with you however in the sentiment which you uttered at our last meeting that whatever may be the perplexity there is no use in our losing our temper on the subject & I felt the justice of your remonstrating on my temporary irritation'.[62]

Another letter, written as Campbell set out on a trip to Scotland, pays more of the same tribute to Colburn. Campbell assures him 'that I shall mention your name in the north as one of the most honourable men I have to deal with & one of the best friends I possess'.[63] As late as 1842, years after Campbell had left the *New Monthly*, he and Colburn were still exchanging friendly missives.

Tact and geniality can only go so far in making employees (which is what Campbell was) feel valued. Payment is also a factor. Colburn's relations with Campbell and other contributors were predicated on business matters and

---

[60] Redding, op cit., I, 163–5.
[61] National Art Library, F.48.E.11, 40–41.
[62] National Art Library, F.48.E.11, 78–79.
[63] National Art Library, F.48.E.11, 66–67.

it was his practice to pay generously. When a book sold unexpectedly well, Colburn would sometimes give the author a bonus on top of the agreed fee for the copyright; Matthew Rosa documents ex gratia payments for Theodore Hook, Horace Smith, and Lady Morgan. They were not the only beneficiaries.

COLBURN AMONG THE VAMPYRES

A balanced assessment of Colburn requires one to take notice, as has just been argued, of his admirable professional qualities. There are, however, manifest misdoings which should also go into one's final judgement on him. One such misdoing—centred on the *New Monthly*—is particularly scandalous and wholly typical: the 'Vampyre' affair. It reflects badly on Colburn, although one has to admire what, in contemporary terms, would be called his *chutzpah*.

One picks up the narrative in the epochal (for Colburn) year, 1816, when Colburn published his hallmark novel— the primal 'silver fork' text, Lady Caroline Lamb's *Glenarvon*. The other factor is bad weather and what came of it.

The unprecedentedly wet summer of 1816 and the inconvenience it caused a party of distinguished literary tourists (Lord Byron, Percy Shelley, Mary Godwin, Claire Clairmont and John Polidori) is legendary. Novels have been written and films made about the creative consequences of the incessant rain that summer. Climatically, the bad weather began, far away, in Indonesia, with the eruption of Mount Tambora. It hit seven on the Volcanic Explosivity Index, making it the largest such event in a thousand years. The result, worldwide, was the 'year without a summer' and a less deadly eruption of Gothicism in Villa Diodati, alongside Lake Geneva, where the English tourists and *littérateurs* were staying. Pent up by the foul weather, they beguiled the rainy days and nights with light reading and a competition to write the most spine-chilling ghost story which their bored, and highly creative, minds could come up with.

Mary Godwin (soon to be Mary Shelley) was evidently struck by the fact that Milton had once resided in Villa Diodati. She elected to rewrite *Paradise Lost* as *Frankenstein*. Shelley and Byron rather fizzled out: literature was, in the final analysis, more than a parlour game for them. None the less, as a striking entry in Polidori's diary, for 18 June, testifies, they remained receptive listeners: 'L[ord] B[yron] repeated some verses of Coleridge's *Christabel*, of the witch's breast; when silence ensued, and Shelley, suddenly shrieking and putting his hands to his head, ran out of the room with a candle. Threw water on his face, and after gave him ether. He was looking at Mrs. S[helley], and suddenly thought of a woman he had heard of who had eyes instead of nipples, which, taking hold of his mind, horrified him.'[64]

The author of 'The Vampyre', Doctor Polidori was, like the eighteen-year-old Mary, young—barely twenty. The two of them got on well. A graduate of Edinburgh medical school (the youngest ever to qualify, supposedly), Polidori had learned his sawbone trade (which he despised) on cadavers supplied by Edinburgh's famous, so-called 'resurrectionists'—a grim joke. Medical science needed corpses: the gallows and the stillborn (the only legitimate supply) were inadequate. Neither would rotting cadavers do. Anatomists needed 'fresh' meat – still warm, ideally – and, in a world without refrigeration, a constant supply of such bodies. Burke and Hare, the most notorious of the resurrectionists solved the demand-and-supply problem by murder. Their colleagues in the resurrection trade, like Victor Frankenstein, dug up what the gravediggers had buried only a few hours earlier.

Polidori had written his thesis on 'somnambulism'. He was fascinated by the paranormal. A second-generation Italo-Englishman, he was handsome, politically radical,

---

[64] See, for the whole episode, William Michael Rossetti, ed., *The Diary of Dr. John William Polidori, 1816, relating to Byron, Shelley, etc.* (New York, 2009).

and a vibrant (if rather too talkative) conversationalist.

Polidori had found himself at the Villa Diodati by a once-in-a-lifetime stroke of luck. Byron, immersed in sexual scandal, had decided that England was too hot for him. He would decamp and he needed a travelling companion—preferably a physician. Byron was taken with Polidori, whom he had met socially. The young man was recruited for the duration of the tour abroad, on a handsome stipend of £500. Polidori was flattered to the point of intoxication. Byron's closest friend, John Cam Hobhouse, loathed 'Polly-Wolly' and sowed as much distrust as he could. It was unnecessary. The young medic soon got on Byron's nerves and things were not helped by 'The Vampyre'. Clearly the hero of that short tale, Lord Ruthven, *is* Byron. 'Ruthven' was the title of the noble character, Clarence de Ruthven, Lord Ruthven in *Glenarvon*, which came out in May 1816. Published, of course, to huge *éclat* by Henry Colburn.

It's a certainty there was a copy of *Glenarvon* at the Villa, that everyone had read or dipped into it, and that it was a topic of conversation. It was Lamb, a discarded mistress, who described Byron as 'mad, bad, and dangerous to know'. He, with studied insouciance, dismissed *Glenarvon* as so much drivel. Whether he wanted to pay young 'Polly' £500 p.a. for his tale was something else. Intended as flattery, Polidori's story was tactless and clumsy.

The plot of 'The Vampyre' is simple. The sinister Lord Ruthven takes the handsome young Aubrey on a continental tour with him. On his travels, Ruthven cold-bloodedly destroys every young person who comes his way. Finally, having sucked Aubrey dry, he turns his dead, grey, irresistible eye on Aubrey's sister:

> Aubrey's weakness increased; the effusion of blood produced symptoms of the near approach of death. He desired his sister's guardians might be called, and when the midnight hour had struck, he related composedly what the reader has perused – he died immediately after.

> The guardians hastened to protect Miss Aubrey; but
> when they arrived, it was too late. Lord Ruthven had
> disappeared, and Aubrey's sister had glutted the thirst
> of a VAMPYRE!

No need to call for the ether. One's spine is obstinately
unchilled. Byron had soon had more of the young man than
he could stand and sent him on his way to cross the Alps,
alone, friendless and penniless. On his return to England,
Polidori drifted, gambled wildly, and suffered a disastrous
head injury in a coach accident in 1818, which exacerbated
a temperamental disposition towards melancholy.

'The Vampyre' went into oblivion (*Frankenstein*, too,
for a while, before rising from the grave). Enter Colburn
again. He was infatuated with Byron and things Byronic.
Virtually every copy of the *New Monthly* contained
something connected with the mad, bad lord. He was, for
the publisher, at the zenith of Byron's public notoriety,
the celebrity of celebrities. Byronism is infused into any
number of his silver fork three-deckers.

Lord Byron was naturally disdainful of publishers of
Colburn's kind and worked exclusively with the more
congenial publisher, John Murray. As Byron pithily told
Murray, 'what is not published by you is not written by
me'—words which must have been treasured by the
publisher.[65] But, in 1819, Colburn struck the mother lode.
He claimed that he had a genuine Byronic article. Not
something *about* Byron, but actually and sensationally *by*
Byron. The timing was perfect, as *Glenarvon* was by now in
multiple reprinting, flying off his library shelves and from
his printers' (Sherwood, Neely and Jones) warehouse.

Colburn originally, and with deliberate vagueness, claimed
that 'The Vampyre' had been passed to him by someone
familiar with the events at Villa Diodati: Countess Breuss, a
Russian aristocrat, resident in Geneva. She had, evidently,

---

[65] *Letters*, 15 May 1819.

formed a close association with Polidori. In his diary, Polidori records that she had two husbands: 'one in Russia, one at Venice'. Divorce (which one?) was proving tricky. In Russia, she had performed in theatricals for Catherine. She was evidently helpful in getting Polidori back to England, after his relationship with Byron broke down.[66]

In 1818, Colburn claimed, Breuss passed on to him a bundle of manuscripts, with the comment that he might care to 'peruse these *ébauches* of so great genius [as Byron] and those under his influence'. Indeed, he did. The bundle contained a complete copy of 'The Vampyre'. 'Peruse' or 'purchase'? In the murk generated by this episode, other accounts claim that the manuscript came to Colburn from an 'unknown correspondent'. Unlikely. What is tantalizingly unknowable is whether Breuss was acting under secretive instruction from Polidori.

In the April 1819 *New Monthly*, Polidori's fifteen-thousand-word story (a hefty item by the journal's normal standards) came out prefaced by a clearly confected article, 'Extract of a letter from Geneva'. A party of English tourists are described visiting the villa, attempting to relive the exciting events of three years earlier, the wet summer, the eruption of literary creativity. They meet the Countess Breuss—a confidante of Polidori, who brings the whole episode to life. The account supplies details which were to become legendary, via the string of biographies of the Villa Diodati party.

It seems most likely that Polidori actually wrote this

---

[66] The account here is indebted to Andrew McConnell Stott's 'The Poet, the Physician and the Birth of the Modern Vampire', https://publicdomainreview.org/2014/10/16/the-poet-the-physician-and-the-birth-of-the-modern-vampire/ and, as regards the transmission of 'The Vampyre' manuscript to Colburn, James Rieger, 'Dr. Polidori and the Genesis of *Frankenstein*', *Studies in English Literature 1500–1900*, (Winter 1963). Rieger, it should be noted, is skeptical about the 'horror competition' legend.

cache of materials for Breuss. But—fatefully—he did not claim authorship. Perhaps he was too frightened of Byron to do so. 'The Vampyre' came out in the magazine (without any preliminary consultation of either Byron or Murray) flagrantly titled as being by 'Lord Byron'.

Byron, abroad at this stage of his life, was informed by letter from Murray and by an item in the Paris-based *Galignani's Messenger*. He and Murray were, understandably, furious. But the fog around this episode was brewed thicker by Byron writing to *Galignani's Messenger*, at the end of April, denying authorship but conceding the idea might have been his.

Byron also conceded, publicly, that he had written a fragmentary vampire tale. But it was not 'The Vampyre'. Murray, in a belated attempt to prove the point, appended Byron's vampiric fragment to the publication of *Mazeppa*, later in 1819. He did so, apparently, without Byron's consent ('what do I care about vampires!').

Whatever part he had hitherto played, Polidori was not apparently warned that 'The Vampyre' was imminently to appear in Colburn's magazine, with Byron proclaimed as its author. Nor, apparently, was he (or Byron) remunerated. As soon as he saw the magazine, Polidori wrote to Colburn in protest:

> I received a copy of the magazine of last April and am sorry to find that your Genevan correspondent has led you into a mistake with regard to the tale of *The Vampyre*—which is not Lord Byron's but was written entirely by me at the request of a lady.[67]

He evidently wanted, in addition to public correction, due payment.

---

[67] See M. Gibson, *Dracula and the Eastern Question: British and French Vampire Narratives of the Nineteenth-Century Near East* (New York, 2006), pp. 18–20.

Colburn declined to give any definite response on paper. He went round in person to Covent Garden, where Polidori was staying, a few days after 'The Vampyre' was published in the magazine. In conversation, he offered £300, plus contract, plus an *amende* to be printed in the May issue of the magazine if Polidori dropped all his threats to publicize or bring an injunction.

A fooled Polidori agreed verbally—after which Colburn went to ground. Whenever, in the days thereafter, Polidori called at the publisher's office, he was 'out'. The magazine was meanwhile reprinting—no issue of the *New Monthly* had sold as fast or as numerously. Colburn had also set in motion a volume edition to be published by Sherwood, Neely and Jones, impudently entitled *The Vampyre: A Tale by the Right Honourable Lord Byron*. By now Colburn must have realized that he was perpetrating a gross fraud.

Polidori found himself in the exquisitely embarrassed position of being unable to prove he owned the copyright. There was no registration at Stationers' Hall. The Countess Breuss's testimony would not stand up in a British court. He was compromised.[68]

In the prefatory letter from Geneva there were references to 'Dr —.' Knowing readers would pick up the clear implication: Dr Polidori was in cahoots with Colburn and the current editor of the *New Monthly,* Alaric Watts.

Colburn's fall-back line of defence, now and later, was that 'The Vampyre' was Byron's 'idea' and Polidori was merely the secretary or conduit. In the May issue of the magazine, Polidori wrote an explanation along the same slippery lines. The seminal 'idea' was the poet's; his contribution had been merely to transcribe. Later book editions buy into this obfuscation with the title: *The Vampyre: A Tale Related by Lord Byron to John Polidori.*

It was all sham. The responsible editor of the *New Monthly*

---

[68] The full account of this murky episode is given in D. L. Macdonald, *Poor Polidori* (Toronto: University of Toronto Press, 1991).

(22-year-old Alaric Watts) suspected the whole thing had been cooked up by Colburn and Polidori (and possibly Breuss). He resigned his editorial post to 'exculpate' himself.

Various accounts testify that Polidori had to make do with a paltry £30 ex gratia payment (it could have originated in a misheard joke about thirty pieces of silver—the traitor's payment). Clarifications came late in the day, after Colburn had made a mint of money. The reading public did not care about intricacies of authorship. 'The Vampyre' was taken to be a shameless self-portrait by the world's most ruthless womanizer (a founding member of the 'League of Incest').

With Byron's name (falsely) attached to it, or dragged behind it, the 'trashy tale' was sensationally popular. Five book-editions came out in 1819 alone. There were translations (pirated) in Europe, dramatic adaptations, and an opera. There was nothing new about vampires as such, but the literary effect of 'The Vampyre' was momentous. It not only inspired but forever 'Byronised' the genre.

Two careers were ruined by 'The Vampyre' episode: those of Polidori (who would now trust him as an author?) and Watts (who would now trust him as an editor?). Polidori died aged twenty-five, in 1821, suicidally depressed, and probably by a self-administered dose of prussic acid.

Yours ever
W. Jerdan

THE EDITOR OF THE LITERARY GAZETTE

THE LITERARY GAZETTE

Three years into his proprietorship of the *New Monthly Magazine*, Colburn embarked on another journalistic experiment, more momentous, in terms of literary culture, than its predecessor.

In 1817, following German prototypes, he set up the *Literary Gazette* as the first serious 1s weekly review of books in Britain. Colburn's venal hand lies heavily on its early issues: the first, for instance, has an article toadying to his Royal Highness the Prince Regent, and an 'Ode on a Prospect of Almack's Assembly Rooms' ('Ye Spacious Rooms! Ye Folding Doors!'). The journal, readers are informed, 'is expressly designed for the polite circles.' It was as expressly designed to puff Colburn's books to those circles. The subsequent evolution of the paper is the history of editorial rebellion against proprietorial interferences. Shades of things to come.

After six months (by which time a circulation of around 3,000 was being claimed), William Jerdan bought a third share, and another third was taken by Longmans (evidently Colburn at the time was suffering one of his periodic cash-flow crises). In 1819, another blow for the paper's liberation from Colburn was struck when he ceased to be its publisher. An editorial of 17 June 1820 declared, defiantly, that 'literary critical independence cannot … coexist with the circumstance of booksellers having a property in a review'. Fighting words. The *Gazette* demonstrated its independence in 1821 by slashing Lady Morgan's *Italy*—a cut so painful that Colburn actually stopped advertising in the paper for a month or two afterwards.

MAGAZINERY WITHOUT THE DRAMA

As the vehicles for the biggest names and juiciest scandals, the *New Monthly Magazine* and the *Literary Gazette* have commandeered most of the attention given to Colburn's periodical ventures. In some ways, however, two less glamorous journals associated with the height of his career reveal a great deal more about Colburn's genuine business acumen. First, in 1829, he bought the monthly *Naval and Military Magazine,* promptly relaunched as the *United Service Journal.*

This serious publication for Britain's large population of active and retired servicemen seems an odd choice for London's most fashionable publisher. Upon closer examination, however, we find that officers of both services would inevitably have been drawn from the same upper-middle and upper classes that populated (and read) the pages of Colburn's other publications. By the same token, civilian members of these classes would have known or been related to servicemen and thus had at least a latent interest in matters military and naval. The *United Service Journal* explicitly stated, in the first issue under Colburn's proprietorship, that it hoped to be of interest to the general public.[69] Ultimately, it was aimed at the usual Colburnian carriage trade.

In his chapter on the military in *Victorian Periodicals*

---

[69] Jan. 1829, 2.

and Victorian Society, Albert Tucker not only acknowledges the affiliation of officers with fashionable society, but also perceives a connection between military periodicals and fashionable literature. He notes that, in Colburn's day, 'serious military subjects tended to be more than balanced by memoirs, semi-fictional tales, and anecdotes in which the authors sought, in their style and choice of subject, to imitate writers of silver-fork fiction'[70]. Indeed, the *United Service Journal,* even in its earliest issues, featured writing by Colburn's authors (including a translation by Jane Porter, author of *Thaddeus of Warsaw*) and excerpts from his books (such as the three-volume *Naval Sketch Book*). With only minimal changes in presentation, this material could have appeared in his *New Monthly* or *Court Journal.*

The magazine also contrived to engage with serious issues and offer genuinely useful information. Its articles and letters to the editor featured, for example, a debate on the use of brevet ranks that continued over a period of years. It annually recorded the distribution of the army and of the navy, listing regiments and ships, their commanders, and their locations. Each month the journal included an almanac of promotions, births, marriages, and deaths of officers. Moreover, the *United Service Journal's* very appearance appealed to lovers of military precision: with its single-columned text, wide margins, and high-quality illustrations (all typical of its original printers, the Bentley brothers), it looked more like a fine book than a periodical. Circulation figures are not available, but as it was the only monthly military periodical in Britain until the 1850s, we can assume that Colburn derived all the usual benefits of a monopoly. Its success is also attested by its longevity: Colburn rechristened it the *United Service Magazine and Naval and Military Journal* in 1842 and gave it up altogether on his retirement in 1853, but it lasted into the twentieth century.

---

[70] P. 63.

That Colburn had a sure touch with the military market was further demonstrated in 1833 when he founded a weekly periodical to complement his monthly *United Service Journal*. Tucker is practically the only scholar to acknowledge Colburn's hand in the establishment of the *Naval and Military Gazette* and he is also singularly generous in recognizing 'the serious professional intent of the publisher' behind both magazines.[71] Colburn's seriousness was, Tucker believes, shown most clearly by his hiring Sir John Philippart as editor of the *Naval and Military Gazette* from the time of its foundation and of the *United Service Magazine* from its 1842 relaunch. Philippart had not only worked at the War Office but also had experience in editing a similar periodical (the *Military Panorama*), and he was given the freedom to join the drive for reform that marked so many military circles.[72] The contrast between Philippart and Campbell or Bulwer is most striking—and indicative of how accurately Colburn perceived the differing needs and expectations of his audiences. *The Naval and Military Gazette* not only provided a good return on Colburn's investment but also outlived him, finally merging with another periodical in 1886.

'Henry Colburn, therefore, owned and directed two of the most important military periodicals in Britain for twenty-six years'—quite an accomplishment for a man often belittled for his light literature and compulsion to puff.[73] And this was not an anomalous or even unusual direction for the publisher, but a typically perceptive filling of a gap in what was already his market.

---

[71] P. 66.

[72] Ibid.

[73] Ibid., 65.

THE PRINCE OF PUFFERS: A DEFENCE

It is appropriate here to add a few more words in defence of Colburn. He was, it is fair to say, the first publisher to appreciate how creatively and mutually beneficial it could be to play a two-handed game as the producer of books and the conductor (whether as editor or proprietor or part-owner) of magazines.

Over the nearly half-century of his publishing career, he would hold some share in no fewer than nine periodicals. Various sources mention his involvement with yet more periodicals but the proof remains elusive.[74] Those with which he was demonstrably involved are, in chronological order, the *New Monthly Magazine;* the *New British Theatre;* the *Literary Gazette;* the *Sunday Times;* the *Quarterly Journal of Science, Literature, and Art;* the *Athenaeum;* the *Court Journal;* the *United Service Journal;* and the *Naval and Military Gazette*. No publisher in the century had his finger in so many magazine pies.

What he did with those fingers is summed up in a single pejorative word. Charges of 'puffery' were thrown at virtually every move by Colburn in the periodicals market. They have dogged his reputation ever since. Yet, closely examined, puffery is a vague and problematic objection, its deleteriousness is a far more subjective matter than is

---

[74] Duncan Wu, for example, notes in *William Hazlitt: The First Modern Man* (2009) that Colburn had a part interest in the magazine *John Bull*.

usually conceded, and Colburn's involvement with it has most frequently been decried by those with an axe to grind or a similarly pointed agenda.

Perhaps worst of all among these critics and criticisms was *Fraser's Magazine's* mock-tribute, 'Thou shalt live for ever, as Prince Paramount of Puffers and Quacks'.[75] That prophecy has proven all too accurate. The caricature of Colburn as the 'prince of puffers' has been perpetuated by so many other sources and has endured longer, and more injuriously, than any other memorial. One has to grant that Colburn was indeed a puffer of the first order, while protesting that puffery is by no measure the sum total of what he did and what he achieved in his fifty-year career.

The *Oxford English Dictionary* defines puffery, in its usual stuffy way, as 'inflated laudation, esp[ecially] by way of advertisement', while a puffer is 'one who extols a person or thing in inflated terms, and usually for some interested reason'. For a publisher, it might take the form of ensuring good reviews—or biased 'notices', as they were often called—for his books, either in his own magazines or in other magazines made friendly by the purchase of legitimate advertising within their pages. Puffs could also masquerade as teasers or other comments about a publisher's titles in the literary intelligence columns that were a standard feature of these periodicals. By making readers think that these were judicious editorial opinions rather than covert advertisements, the claims made for these books appeared to be genuine and, therefore, independent. As Colburn (a master of the art) practiced it, puffery extended beyond these formal definitions to include a whole range of publicity stunts—some outrageous but, most of them, effective in selling his wares. A really clever publisher (and none was cleverer than Colburn) would create a controversy surrounding a book or journal to whip up interest in it, or perhaps indulge in intertextual

---

[75] *Fraser's*, Apr. 1830, 320.

S. T. Coleridge

AUTHOR OF "CHRISTABEL."

puffery, mentioning one of his magazines in one of his books or vice versa. One suspects Colburn enjoyed his virtuosity. He had every right to.

Without excusing behaviour on the weak grounds that 'everyone else does it', if a practice is so widespread as to be commonplace and even universal, then no one practitioner can justly be singled out for engaging in it. Yet this injustice is what happened to Henry Colburn. Puffery was common, and winked at, in the book trade long before he was even born (whenever that might have been). The *Oxford English Dictionary* traces the use of 'puff' in the publishing sense of the word back to the 1730s—and by Colburn's time, it was routine among both authors and publishers. This is hardly surprising: the many book writers who also contributed to journals were perfectly positioned to construct favourable reviews of their friends' publications or, should the need arise, their own.

That this occurred with even with eminent literary figures is made clear by Robert Southey's letter to Samuel Taylor Coleridge of 12 February 1808, in which he cries, 'Puff me, Coleridge! if you love me, puff me! Puff a couple of hundreds into my pocket!'.[76] This, however, was mere histrionics on Southey's part—Coleridge had already proven his love by publishing a frankly puffing review of Southey's *Espriella* in the *Courier*. So, too, when the poet L. E. L. wrote a panegyric on Bulwer's career in the *New Monthly* and he returned the compliment with a glowing review of her *Romance and Reality*, it was nothing new or noteworthy.[77] These latter instances just happened to involve personages somewhat less august than Southey and to occur under the jurisdiction of Henry Colburn.

Colburn was by no means the only publisher overseeing and instigating campaigns of puffery. Nor was Colburn the only *quality* publisher to sully his hands with the

---

[76] Erickson, 96.

[77] Adburgham, 179–81.

practice. Most of his rivals practised the same black art—or allowed it—in some degree.[78] To take one example of many: John Taylor, of the firm of Taylor and Hessey, is routinely portrayed and remembered as the quintessential gentleman publisher, yet, on occasion, Taylor personally puffed his authors—using no less a medium than his *London Magazine.* Taylor wrote the article 'A Visit to John Clare, with a Notice of His New Poems' and published it in the *London's* November 1821 issue, contemporaneously with Clare's new poems. When Erickson refers to this case, he tellingly calls it 'direct marketing', not puffery, which is a euphemism too far, one might think.[79] One should also note that Taylor actually came out and said what one suspects Colburn only dared think; he wrote to his brother James on 28 April 1821 that owning the *London* brought 'the Advantages of a public Situation equal to a perpetual Advertisement'.[80]

One of the reasons publishers practised puffery, aside from the obvious sales 'advantages' to be gained thereby, was that they felt keenly the limitations of the standard advertising methods of the time, which consisted almost solely of placing small print ads in magazines and in the backs of other books. These were scarcely advertisements as such, usually just dull announcements that such and such a new title had been published and was available from such and such a bookseller or circulating library. They were sufficient for many books, particularly non-fiction titles from which no great sale was expected, and Colburn himself was among those who used such 'notices' extensively, frequently leading off his *New Monthly Magazine* with six or eight pages listing them. Other books, however, he judged to need more help. This was particularly the case

---

[78] Rosa, op cit., 19.

[79] Erickson, op cit., 195–6.

[80] Tim Chilcott, *A Publisher and His Circle: The Life and Work of John Taylor, Keats's Publisher,* p. 134.

with novels of the day, which had only their come-on title and (hopefully) known author to recommend them. When the author was an unknown or chose to remain anonymous, the situation was more fraught. As Colburn's publications increasingly were by unknown or unrecognized writers, he increasingly resorted to other measures to bring them to the public's attention.

The trend-setting books that became his specialty in the 1820s, notably silver-fork novels and memoirs of fashionable life and travel, required no-holds-barred publicity campaigns that would ensure a large initial sale before the books began their almost inevitable descent into obscurity after one or two seasons—or word of mouth talked them down.

Fortunately, Colburn was never short of ingenious ideas when it came to publicity. He is thought, for example, to have been the first publisher with a dedicated advertising department, a development which appalled the high-Tory gents at *Fraser's:* 'Does he not', they asked sarcastically, 'keep clerks and writers whose exclusive employ is, as he says, "solely to look after the papers and advertisements"?'.[81] Indeed, he did, and he had no reason, commercially, to be ashamed of it.

The simplest and most direct means of puffery that Colburn and his advertising department had at their disposal was, inevitably, the printing of favourable reviews in his magazines. Stirring his own pot. He did this to varying degrees in all of his journals, but it is a rare issue when the works of other publishers do not get some space—and sometimes even good reviews. Of course, this is not proof positive of impartially ethical reviewing. There were other pressures on independent critical judgement. One cannot but notice that Murray, in particular, took out many paid advertisements in Colburn's periodicals and came away with good notices as well. It was for Albemarle

---

[81] *Fraser's*, Apr. 1830, 319.

Street money well spent. But if other publishers were, essentially, paying for good reviews, Colburn could hardly be expected scrupulously to refrain from puffing his own works, particularly in the *Literary Gazette* and *Court Journal*.

Colburn, it must be conceded, sometimes got a little carried away and puffed titles to audiences with no direct interest in them. A prime example of this occurs in the *United Service Journal,* wherein appears a notice for the Standard Novels, the monthly reprint series launched by Colburn and Bentley in 1831. It delivers its hyperbolic verdict on the first four titles in the series:

> We cannot speak in terms of too high praise of this design, nor of the manner in which the spirited publishers are performing their part of it. [...] Here then we have in three volumes the condensed (not abridged) matter of nine, most neatly printed with frontispiece and vignettes, of most convenient size, and also most conveniently cheap. We can add no stronger recommendation of the Standard Novels.[82]

It certainly is hard to conceive of a stronger recommendation than this—nor one more likely to miss any conceivable target.

Yet circulating subtler literary intelligence was another art deftly practised by Colburn. One of the more amusing, and least repeated, anecdotes about this branch of puffery is related by Cyrus Redding in his *Fifty Years' Recollections:*

> When Horace Smith published "Brambletye House" I went down to Brighton to see him, and among other things, remarked that one of the newspapers had said pic-nic parties were continually made up to visit the remains of that old place. The paragraph had the simplicity and air of truth to characterise it. When I

---

[82] *United Service Journal,* Apr. 1831, 240.

came back to town I told Colburn I had seen Mr. Smith,
who was equally pleased with myself at the intelligence.
The paragraph, I found, had been concocted in town,
and sent to the country papers by the publisher. I
allowed I was taken in by an unworthy practice.[83]

Since Colburn's ingenious puff about picnicking readers,
'unworthy' as it may have been, managed to deceive one of
his editors and the author himself of the work in question,
one can only imagine its success with readers.

For an entrepreneur with a knack for publicity and a raft
of publications pulsing out regularly, it was only a matter
of time before Colburn hit upon the idea of using these
publications to promote each other. It was normal for
one journal to refer to another or even for a fashionable
novel to refer to a fashionable journal. But, of course, no
other publisher in London had so well stocked a hand with
which to play this game as Colburn (proprietor as he was
of so many journals, publisher as he was of so many works
of popular fiction).

Colburn frequently exercised this easy option of
scratching each other's backs, but also came up with
more complex gimmicks. One such was the reprinting
in the *Court Journal* of a letter from Thomas Campbell to
Thomas Moore correcting an anecdote in Moore's recently
published, and bestselling, biography of Lord Byron
(published by Murray, of course). The date of the letter
was 18 February 1830, the date of the magazine was the
following Saturday, and the *Court Journal* stated itself to
be sure that 'our readers will thank us, on more than one
account, for using an opportunity which presented itself, of
intercepting the following copy' of Campbell's letter (italics
in original). Since Campbell never complained about the
interception, it is fair to conclude that this was the inside
job it appears to be. The editor of the *New Monthly* shared

---

[83] Redding, op cit., II, 345.

an exclusive document with a sister journal and reaped the reward of having his point of view set in print. Colburn had one journal with a scoop, another with a bit of subtle but free publicity, and at least, one can deduce, one happy editor.

While conceding that Colburn was an unabashed puffer, one must go on to consider why he, in particular, was so stigmatised for what others were doing as well. It is true that puffery was an inherently deceitful practice, but was it less reprehensible when Taylor or others in the book trade did it? Colburn puffed on a grander scale than anyone else, but this alone cannot account for the singular obloquy that he received. The reason, one concludes, is not that he puffed more than others or that he did it over such a long period or in so many different ways, but that he puffed more successfully than anyone else did, try as they might. Colburn's puffery not only drew the attention of his competitors—and their imitation—but also made them angrily jealous. Unable to beat him at his own game, they resorted to talking him down.

Colburn's detractors naturally included his competitors in the periodicals market. Thus, the *Noctes Ambrosianae* series—the hugely successful conversations over plentiful drink by fictionalised versions of the *Blackwood's Edinburgh Magazine* staff (John Lockwood, James Hogg, et al.)— vituperated his 'shameful and shameless puffery' even while admitting that the publisher was an 'enterprising' man with a sense of 'honour'.[84] The *Westminster Review* took a similarly conflicted line. Rather less inclined to acknowledge Colburn's good points were magazines such as the *Athenaeum* and the aforementioned *Fraser's*, which exulted in the self-righteousness of not being associated with any book publishers (or 'popular' books, in *Fraser's* case) and, therefore, beyond any accusations of the malign practice of puffery. Fraser's most egregious comments on

---

[84] *Blackwood's Edinburgh Magazine*, July 1826, 98.

Colburn's puffery already have been cited, but these are just the tip of the iceberg. One particularly extravagant critique was constructed around Colburn and Bentley's latest novel by Bulwer, then the editor of the *New Monthly*— and *Fraser's* (and their star contributor Thackeray's) *bête noire:*

> Turn we to *Paul Clifford,* which his booksellers, in their usual way of puffing,—directly, indirectly, obliquely, diagonally, transversely,—have cried up as the most extraordinary production that this, or any other country, in times bygone, or in times present, or times to come, have, are, or will be favoured with. The praise of puffing it might be supposed can no farther go; but we shall see that, when the author honours the world with his next performance.[85]

There is little doubt that the underlying cause of *Fraser's* vexation was that, thanks in part to the puffery, the first impression of *Paul Clifford*—the largest first impression of any modern novel—sold out on the day of publication.[86] The *Athenaeum*, too, resorted to crude satire when it parodied Colburn as 'Colophon' on its front page.[87] Its hostility against Colburn continued for years.

Rosa notes that it was not merely rival publishers who attacked Colburn's promotional techniques: 'writers, especially those whose books were not published by Colburn, loved to make slighting references to his puffery'.[88] One could easily enough attribute the spiteful anecdotes and lampoons of Colburn to a motley crew of aggrieved contemporaries composed of various writers and editors.

---

[85] *Fraser's Magazine,* June 1830, 526.

[86] Alison Adburgham, *Silver Fork Society: Fashionable Life and Literature from 1814 to 1840,* p. 160.

[87] 1 July 1829.

[88] Op. cit., 190–1.

W. M. Thackeray's extended parody of Colburn and Bentley in *Pendennis* (discussed below), strongly supports this view, since in this case we know the particulars of his grievance.

Many of Colburn's own authors commented, sharply, on their publisher's puffery, especially his more blatant or elaborate antics, but most recognized and appreciated that his ingenious (if occasionally unscrupulous) advertising gave their works the best possible chance of succeeding. It was generally only those whose efforts for his firm did not succeed—or who could not get their works published by Colburn at all—who took the hardest moral line against puffery.

The anger and envy felt by Colburn's competitors and disgruntled contributors was compounded by his seeming utterly indifferent to their complaints. They never seemed to touch him. He kept on doing it, whatever the complaints and from whichever source they came. He continued his puffery throughout his lengthy career. And when he directly refers to puffery (as in the letter to Bentley quoted below), he is wholly unapologetic. Colburn's insouciance is further displayed in a 9 December 1836 letter to Benjamin Disraeli concerning some harsh criticism of the author's *Henrietta Temple*, 'which', he says consolingly, 'need not therefore give you any more concern than it does me, which is very little indeed. I have no fears for the success of the book'.[89] This last line is the giveaway: as long as his books sold, it did not matter to the publisher what his critics and competitors said about them or him. What he writes here to Disraeli is the archetypal Colburnian declaration of belief in himself.

One can understand why jealous competitors and writers berated Colburn's puffing ways and his 'cheerful disrespect for their dignified conception of business-methods'.[90] It is

---

[89] Hughenden Papers, 235/3, 25–26.
[90] Sadleir Papers, op cit., 360, 8.

harder to understand why later, perceptive, commentators further blackened the publisher's already tarnished name. Sadleir is only the most obvious and vitriolic among them. In *XIXth-Century Fiction,* he is forced to concede Colburn's 'daring and intelligence', but launches much more energetically into how the merchandiser of Burlington Street 'debauched the critics and put them on his pay-sheet'. Even more revealing is the contrast Sadleir draws between Colburn—'a book-manufacturer, not a publisher'—and Richard Bentley, 'the serious-minded craftsman-booklover'. Without stopping to challenge this characterization of Bentley, we can see that Sadleir's problem with Colburn actually stems from his distaste for the modern, businesslike approach to publishing. A gentleman publisher himself, Sadleir naturally prefers publishers in the earlier, more gentlemanly mode, employing their fine taste to support worthy men of letters, regardless of the financial consequences.

Sadleir's manuscript reflections on Colburn conclude that, 'above all he realised the power of ballyhoo at a time when ostentation was considered smart and so- called Society mistook for health and gaiety what was really the flush and excitement of a transient fever'.[91] One apprehends from this haughty dismissal that Colburn's clientele did not live up to Sadleir's standards either. The book trade was a fallen world—and Colburn one of the prime architects of that fall. It's a dubious verdict, objectionable on a number of fronts.

Recent commentators have distanced themselves from the familiar charges made against Colburn, primarily by recontextualizing his puffery into the larger machineries of British publishing. As far back as 1928, Collins recognized him as a 'prophet of the modern spirit'[92] of advertising, and indeed, one cannot see a publisher's press

---

[91] Sadleir Papers, 360, 11–12.

[92] Op cit., 192.

release or hear about authors writing their own 'reader reviews' on Amazon.com without being reminded that Colburn blazed a trail through this territory nearly two centuries ago. It could be argued that, as regards his more extravagant feats of 'puffing' (what is now called 'hype), Colburn's main offence was merely to be a century ahead of his time.[93] A few writers are convinced that he was so far ahead—and therefore so close to modern practice—as to be a 'genius'.[94] Thus, opinion has come full circle and gone from deriding Colburn for his puffery to elevating him above his contemporaries because of it.

---

[93] "Henry Colburn, Publisher," 80.

[94] For example, Wilson, *Byromania,* 79; Erickson, op cit., 152.

CRISIS

Colburn's long career is punctuated by crises—and hair-breadth's escapes from them. That of 1819 seems to have been the most serious in his early years. Only four new titles are listed in the *English Catalogue*. The publisher may have lost money in the catastrophic fire at Bensley's, the printer's, in late June of that year. An urgent advertisement of March 1820 asks for the recall of all Colburn's borrowed library books, which suggests the Conduit Street establishment (and its stock of 50,000 volumes) was up for sale.[95] At the same time, Colburn designated himself 'Henry Colburn and Co.' (He kept this style until 1824, when he re-emerged as plain 'Henry Colburn', assuming the '& Co' again as he came to the end of his career, in 1851, before disposing of all his publishing interest to Hurst and Blackett). But, whatever the 1819 crisis, Colburn rode it out and was trading normally in 1820.

---

[95] See Melnyk, op cit., 69–70.

THE FIRST DECADE: SUMMARY

Colburn cut his teeth as a purveyor of circulating library materials, an over-the-counter bookseller and, within a remarkably short period, a publisher of multi-volume books under his own name. It gave him an unrivalled sense of what the market for light reading matter was. But when he disposed of his library interest to Saunders and Otley, and moved to his office in New Burlington Street, publishing books and magazines had become his principal interest.[96]

Between 1814 and 1824 Colburn conducted a dozen magazines (several simultaneously, at some points) and published 135 new titles. They came out at a steady rate of between ten and fifteen titles a year (with the exception of 1819's virtual blank). The bulk of this decade's output is undistinguished and marked by a surprisingly modest proportion of fiction titles (thirty-one out of the total, around three a year). Only a few of Colburn's titles are worth picking from the mass: Benjamin Franklin's *Private Correspondence* (2 vols, 1817, 21s); David Hume's *Private Correspondence* (2 vols, 1817, 21s); Hazlitt's *Table Talk* (2 vols, 1818, 28s); Goethe's *Memoirs* (2 vols, 1824, 24s); and, crowning all, John Evelyn's *Memoirs* (ed. Bray, 2 vols, 1818, 105s 6d).

Evelyn's and Pepys's diaries are, for posterity, Colburn's

---

[96] The lease on New Burlington Street began 25 March 1823.

main claim to publishing respectability. He evidently took on the Evelyn copyright on the advice of his friend, the antiquarian William Upcott. The Pepys copyright reportedly cost him £2,200 after Murray had turned it down. Colburn was again advised by Upcott to publish. He brought out a selective *Memoirs* in 1825 (2 quarto vols, 126s), which omitted about three-quarters of the manuscript. In 1848, he commissioned a third edition that, to renew the copyright, included almost half the diary. The Pepys copyright (together with Evelyn's *Diary* and Garrick's manuscript correspondence) was among the property that Colburn kept until his death in 1855.

Had Colburn died in 1824 he would have been remembered as an interesting, middle-ranking, mostly respectable practitioner of his trade, very much of his time. His later career would form a different image.

COLBURN'S HEYDAY

The years 1825–29 marked Colburn's heyday. In five years, he published 197 books, of which 107 were fiction and 80 of those three-volume novels. The silver-fork genre dominated the fiction list. This splendid (silver indeed) phase of Colburn's career began in 1825 alongside his selling the Conduit Street library to the new firm of Saunders and Otley (whose business character was studiously and successfully based on that of Colburn). From this point on, Colburn was principally a publisher of books and magazines, with his business premises at 8 New Burlington Street. It was a bold step, and very much in character.

SAUNDERS AND OTLEY

The publishing offspring of Colburn, Saunders and Otley merit a short diversion. The transfer of property, practice and good will between the two publishers offers the clearest insight we have into Colburn's everyday office and business practice.

Like Colburn, Saunders and Otley would prove to be a long-lived firm. Their business operation (although it wilted after their highpoint in the 1830s) lasted from 1824 to 1871. Both founders, Simon Saunders (1783–1861) and Edward John Otley (1798–1857), were by then dead. Both were (particularly the senior partner, Saunders), roughly, of the same vintage as Colburn—give or take a few years.

Their firm took off (soaring, at some points, even higher than Colburn) in the early and mid-1830s, with works by Bulwer Lytton and, pre-eminently, their flagship author, 'Captain [Frederick] Marryat', a writer whose career Colburn had launched by taking a chance and publishing the old salt's first novel, *Frank Mildmay* (1829).[97] Whether or not he did so with a bottle of champagne is not recorded.

Marryat (a long-serving Commander, with a distinguished active service record) had taken to fiction in 1829 after a grumpy argument with the Admiralty (he was famously irascible) and disappointment in his attempts to get into

---

[97] Marryat's interesting life is well summarized in a number of places, most concisely in the ODNB.

parliament. The electorate, he discovered, was strangely ungrateful to its hearts of oak heroes.

The captain wrote slapdash, 'manly' tales—as breezy as their subject matter. Nautical fiction, hugely popular in the 1830s and 1840s, would be the Saunders and Otley long suit, as novels of fashionable life were Colburn's.

Following Colburn's two-handed example, Saunders and Otley founded the *Metropolitan Magazine* in 1831 with (who else?) Thomas Campbell as its first editor. He, lazy as ever, was succeeded by Marryat himself who began serializing and excerpting his briny wares in the magazine—to sales success. He ran, as one might say, a tighter ship than his predecessor.

Marryat's assistant editor Edward Howard produced in the magazine's pages, and under Saunders and Otley's imprint, what is often regarded as the best work of fiction in the nautical genre, *Rattlin the Reefer* (1836). It is one of the few nautical bestsellers of the era which have survived to be reprinted and re-read by posterity.[98]

The childless Colburn would never have an 'And Son' attached to his firms' names. Saunders and Otley are the closest he came to filial successors and the establishment of a dynasty. For a while Saunders and Otley advertised themselves as just that—'Successors to Henry Colburn'.

When, precisely, did they 'succeed'? Sadleir, having examined fragmentary evidence, concludes that the relationship predated the actual takeover by several years:

> For a few years during the eighteen-teens, Saunders and Otley [...] were associated with [Colburn] in a lending library; but I can find no evidence that they were also active partners in publishing or any book bearing the three names in a joint imprint. About 1820 the association ended, or rather a formal separation took place between

---

[98] The early nineteenth-century vogue for the nautical novel is well covered in Royal Gettmann's *Victorian Publisher.*

the library and publishing departments. This may be deduced from a Library Catalogue of that date [...]. It shows the premises at 50 Conduit Street as occupied by Colburn & Co, Publishers. But the title page of the catalogue reads: "Catalogue of Saunders and Otley's (late Colburn, Saunders and Otley's) British and Foreign Public Library, Conduit St, Hanover Square etc."[99]

The assumption is that Saunders and Otley, some years before the contractual incorporation (1820 is the strongest likelihood), had assumed management and day-to-day running of the Conduit Street library business, leaving Colburn (always hectically busy) free to publish. This arrangement seems to have worked satisfactorily to all parties until, restless as ever, Colburn moved on to reassume the complete independence he felt he needed.

Leaving Conduit Street—with its massive stock holdings, commercial goodwill, and extensive membership (and all the stored business paperwork)—was legally complex. The Bentley Papers archive includes the lease signed by Colburn for the rental (not purchase) of his new premises in New Burlington Street.[100] The document was co-signed on 9 February 1823 by the other party: Henry, William, and Stephen Dawson. The lease grants residence and use of 8 New Burlington Street, 'Together with the Stables and Coachhouses behind the same leading into Burlington Mews', to Colburn for twenty-eight years from 25 March 1823 (Colburn clearly foresaw a long future for 'Henry Colburn & Co').

One of the Dawsons was a solicitor, of the partnership Dawson, Capron, and Rowley; George Capron lived next door to the property. The landlord's profession is evident in the excessively detailed contract, which lays out Colburn's numerous obligations besides paying his £210 annual

---

[99] Sadleir, op cit., 360, 3–4.

[100] British Library, Add.MS.46632A, 1–2.

rent. These range from insuring the premises for at least £3,000 with the Sun Fire Insurance Office, to repainting the property every three years with two coats of 'good oil paint'.[101] Most interesting is the stern clause designed to ensure that the building looked like the 'property of a gentleman rather than of a shopkeeper.' Colburn would have been entirely happy with that stipulation. His West End customers required nothing less than a gentlemanly establishment. The agreement explicitly forbade the new occupant to 'expose for sale or otherwise any Books or other Goods in the front of the premises near New Burlington Street aforesaid so that the said Premises shall not externally bear the appearance of other than a private residence'. There should be no stalls on the pavement.

As a concession to the fact that Colburn had a business to run, the lease allowed him to affix over the front door—in letters not more than 'two inches high'—his name and the nature of his business (one wonders whether he opted for 'Bookseller' or 'Publisher'). Colburn was, by contractual agreement, allowed to let the front door 'stand open' during business hours. In summer, one presumes. Calf-bound books smell.

Colburn signed up to all of these fussy demands as a small price to pay for a spacious building in a prime Mayfair location—a property as fashionable as his fiction itself aspired to be. Conduit Street (named after some long-forgotten stream) runs through the heart of this exclusive area of London. New Burlington Street, just to its south, is equally well situated, but more discreetly out of the noisy public way. Number 8 had the added attraction of being near the residence of Lady Cork, the most eminent of London's society hostesses. She had moved to 6 New Burlington Street when widowed in 1798 and would remain there till her death in 1840.

---

[101] Colburn's Sun Fire Insurance contract—signed 27 November 1823—is still extant in the London Metropolitan Archives.

In 1823, Burlington Street was exactly where Colburn, his business healthily expanding in the post-war book-trade boom, wanted to be. Since his books continued to carry his Conduit Street imprint throughout 1823 and none of them bears a New Burlington Street imprint until 1824, one can infer he spent the first year of the lease remodelling the new premises (installing counters, shelves, office space), probably moving in, lock stock and barrel, in early 1824.[102] Unsurprisingly, Colburn lived 'over the shop.' It was an address worthy of his rise in life, he must have felt.

Colburn's move to New Burlington Street meant hiring several new members of staff. He almost certainly brought with him some of his Conduit Street employees who would have been familiar with his book and magazine publishing affairs and practices. But expansion of his business meant a larger editorial and clerical staff. Not to mention 'runners' (with stock and post) and delivery boys. The stables and mews at the back of New Burlington Street (given the weight of multi-volume books) would have been used, with a groom and driver in work-day attendance.

Details of whom the publisher hired, and when he hired them, are found in a memoir written by Edward Morgan (no relation either to the librarian with whom Colburn began or his author Lady Morgan). Morgan was a bookkeeper by trade and was employed by Colburn for four years before Bentley joined the business in 1829. He evidently ingratiated himself tactically with the new partner, Bentley, and, after the 1832 split between him and Colburn, remained in New Burlington Street until his retirement in 1858.[103]

Morgan penned his sycophantic memoir after his friendly master Richard Bentley's death in 1871 (which is mentioned in the text), presumably for the private benefit of Richard's successor, George Bentley, a son of

---

[102] Brown 42.

[103] Sadleir Papers, op cit., 357, 16.

the house (and, presumably, another friend). In this revealing memoir, Morgan is unstinting in his praise of the patriarchal Richard Bentley. He coyly stresses his own professional closeness with the publisher and is merciless in his disparagement of Colburn.

Morgan is not reticent about his own merits. He claims, for example, that the wily Colburn continually tried to 'allure' him from Bentley's service[104] and further claims, immodestly, that Bentley's firm would not have experienced its downturn in the 1840s if only he, Morgan, had had a greater role within it. One need not credit that.

There are other things to disbelieve. Notably Morgan's perpetuating the widespread fallacy that Colburn and Bentley broke up entirely because of their personal falling out. They most certainly did fall out, but Colburn's semi-retirement and withdrawal in 1832 had been pre-planned from the very beginning of their 1829 partnership. Morgan should have known the truth of that better than anyone but it did not fit his obsequious portrait of Bentley as the innocent victim of Colburn. Aged seventy, one may charitably assume that his memory failed him.

Other aspects of his recollections of the Colburn ménage are more reliable. Morgan recalls that it was George Dubourg's 'solicitation' that brought him to work for Colburn in September 1825. One can assume that Dubourg had been with the publisher since his removal to New Burlington Street in 1824, if not earlier.[105] He was Colburn's ledger keeper and, as monitor of the finances, enjoyed his employer's complete trust. Late in 1829, when Colburn set up his own offices, independent of those he shared with Bentley, he transferred Dubourg there as an employee accountable to him alone.[106] Immediately after the partnership's dissolution, a lawsuit brought against

---

[104] Sadleir Papers, op cit., 357, 14–16.

[105] Sadleir Papers, op cit., 357, 1.

[106] Sadleir Papers, op cit., 357, 5.

Colburn by Bentley characterized Dubourg as 'a person who is generally employed by the said H[enr]y Colburn as his Agent in all matters relat[in]g to his bus[ines]s of a publisher'.[107] There is definite evidence that Dubourg stayed with Colburn at least until 1835, but he may, in fact, have remained longer.

Charles Ollier had made his name as co-proprietor of a publishing firm with his younger brother James. They had the distinction of publishing some of Keats's and many of Shelley's works but had fallen on hard times and dissolved their firm in 1822, after only five years in business. Morgan claims that Ollier arrived at Colburn's establishment shortly after himself, that is around September 1825.[108] Once there, Ollier distinguished himself as a reader of manuscripts. We find, for example, Colburn eager for his opinion of Thomas Henry Lister's latest tragedy[109] and know that, after reversing Shoberl's negative verdict on Bulwer's *Pelham* (which would have lost Colburn thousands), Ollier was assigned to the difficult author's manuscripts, as a personal editor, from then onwards.[110] (Bulwer's handwriting, incidentally, was notoriously illegible—particularly by candlelight).

The Sadleir papers also confirm that Ollier was one of Colburn's chief puffers. In October 1829, Colburn writes more than once of the need for him to write paragraphs and notices of James Fenimore Cooper's *Borderers*.[111] The puffs were duly served up.

William Hazlitt recalled that Colburn, or Ollier in his stead, would not receive him at the office when he (Hazlitt) was attracting bad publicity.[112] True or false (it rings true),

---

[107] British Library Add.MS.46632A, 177–189.

[108] Sadleir Papers, op cit., 357, 1.

[109] Sadleir Papers, op cit., 348, 19.

[110] Sadleir Papers, op cit., 348, 2.

[111] Sadleir Papers, op cit., 348, 5–6, 18.

[112] P. G. Patmore, *My Friends and Acquaintance*, II, 351.

it confirms that Ollier was the publisher's right-hand man, stepping in for Colburn during his absences with plenipotentiary authority. We can be certain that this was the case in 1830, when it was Ollier, rather than Bentley, whom Colburn delegated to deal with (the awkward) Mary Shelley and William Jerdan.[113] Royal Gettmann is justified in describing Ollier as 'the general handyman in New Burlington Street', though in later years he was more right-hand man than 'handyman'. He stayed in New Burlington Street, with Bentley, after the partnership's dissolution.[114]

It is difficult to know exactly what job description to attach to P. G. Patmore (father of the better-known Coventry Patmore), another of Colburn's office staff. He contributed to the *New Monthly Magazine* from the 1820s, over which period Colburn also published a few of his books; their connection lasted into the 1840s. That Patmore was not just another hack, however, is demonstrated by the fact that he was a confidant of important Colburn writers such as Campbell and Hazlitt. Patmore also appears to have served behind the scenes as a silent editor of Colburn's books—probably for a fee. He later disclosed that he (Patmore) had demanded significant changes to Robert Ward's primal silver-fork novels (founders of the genre) *Tremaine* (1825) and *De Vere* (1827) and had maintained an anonymous correspondence with the equally anonymous author until the second book was published. The glimpses that Morgan's memoir, and other passing references, give are tantalizing: but there is enough to give us a fuller sense of the hustle and bustle of the Colburn office and those who made it a literary London powerhouse.

---

[113] Sadleir Papers, op cit., 348, 1; 349, 2.

[114] Gettmann, op cit., 41.

THE GREAT CRASH: A PERVERSE OPPORTUNITY FOR COLBURN

As it turned out, 1825–26 was an inauspicious year for bold steps such as the move to New Burlington Street. On 14 January 1826, a bill drawn by the eminent house of Constable (publisher of Walter Scott) on their London agents, Hurst and Robinson, was dishonoured.[115] Hurst and Robinson went under for £300,000, paying creditors 1/3d in the pound. Archibald Constable himself failed for £256,000, paying a barely more respectable 2/9d in the pound. His principal author, Scott, who had signed a complex series of accommodation bills, was left personally liable for £86,000.

Meanwhile Constable's great adversary, Murray, had unprecedented financial reverses. Byron—his star author—died in 1824. In January 1826, his ill-conceived attempt to rival *The Times* with a new paper, *The Representative*, failed at an estimated loss of £26,000. A crushing sum in the currency of the time.[116] Although he was not destroyed, Murray seems, under the misfortunes of 1826 and the impending

---

[115] For the calamity this represented for Scott, see John Sutherland, *The Life of Sir Walter Scott* (London, 1994), Chaps. 14–16.

[116] For details see Humphrey Carpenter, *The Seven Lives of John Murray: The Story of a Publishing Dynasty* (London, 2008) and Samuel Smiles, *A Publisher and his Friends* (London, 1891), Vol II, p. 215.

horror of parliamentary reform, to have adopted an even more conservative publishing policy than usual.[117]

Various eyewitnesses and book historians offer drastic descriptions of the short- and long-term effects of the 1826 crash on the book trade and on British letters generally. Colburn figures centrally and unflatteringly. The perceived effects may be summarized under four heads, as follows.

1. The most immediate effect was trade paralysis. 1826, declared Charles Knight, was 'a lost year for business'.[118] Another eyewitness publisher, Alexander Blackwood, reported from London in early 1826: 'nobody is publishing but Colburn'.[119] James Barnes perceives paralysis of longer duration after the immediate shock: 'the economic dislocation, brought about by the financial crisis of 1825–26, certainly destroyed confidence, causing business to be conducted in a mood of caution.'[120] This caution has been linked to the low quality of the literary product of the following decade: 'an interval of mediocrity', F. A. Mumby calls it.[121]

2. It is authoritatively asserted that a large number of British publishers were driven out of business by the 1826 crash. Royal Gettmann refers to 'the tempest of 1825–6 [which] wrecked scores of publishers.'[122] Gettmann does not cite his source but is clearly echoing a remark ascribed to the bookseller Valpy, in T. F. Dibdin's lively book-trade survey, *Bibliophobia:* 'he had braved the tempests of the years 1825–26, when his Brethren were wrecked by dozens'.[123]

---

[117] F. A. Mumby, *The House of Routledge* (London, 1934), p. 3.

[118] C. Knight, *Passages from the Life of Charles Knight* (New York, 1874), p. 281.

[119] Oliphant, Vol II, p. 57

[120] James J. Barnes, *Free Trade in Books* (London, 1967), p. 4.

[121] Op cit.

[122] R. A. Gettman, *A Victorian Publisher* (Cambridge, 1960), p. 18.

[123] T. F. Dibdin, *Bibliophobia: Remarks on the Present Languid and Depressed State of Literature and the Book Trade* (London, 1832), p. 58.

Michael Sadleir perceives a precisely measurable calamity, referring to the 'evil days of 1825–6, which swept away two-thirds of the publishers of the time'.[124] He clearly took his fraction from Richard Bentley (grandson of Colburn's erstwhile partner), who wrote in 1896 that 'the crisis of 1826 paralysed trade and swept away two-thirds of the publishers of the time'.[125]

3. A large structural change is perceived in British publishing after 1826; as Samuel Smiles put it, 'mercantile confidence in the great publishing houses was almost at an end'.[126] An old regime passed—bloodily.

4. 1826 is commonly seen as a historical moment in which a certain kind of inferior publisher comes into his own. That is to say—publishers like Henry Colburn. Henry Curwen, for instance, observes that in the 'paralysis' of 1826: 'Colburn was the only one who still continued his ventures, and from the light and soothing nature of his publications, chiefly fictions calculated to allay the torture of reality, he was able to reap a rich reward for his temerity.'[127] Curwen's source is Charles Knight who, while recording 1826 as a lost year, notes: 'this was the reasoning of most of us, of nearly all, with the exception of Mr Colburn, who pushed his new works with great vigour, having the market of light literature almost to himself.'[128]

'Light literature' is a simplification. Colburn's publishing at this period rests on the tripod of fiction, travel and popular-history works, aimed at the leisured reader. The striking feature of his production is the extraordinarily high cost of his books. Colburn was intimately involved with the

---

[124] *XIXth Century Fiction*, II, p. 214.

[125] R. Bentley, *Some Leaves from the Past Swept Together* (privately printed, London, 1896), pp. 88—92.

[126] Op cit., Vol II, p. 212.

[127] Henry Curwen, *A History of Booksellers* (London, 1873), pp. 255–256.

[128] Knight, p. 277.

top end of the general reading market—borrowers from the country's 500 or so circulating libraries.

The calamitous effects of 1826 became book trade lore, and were grossly exaggerated.[129] There is, however, little doubt that the 'crash' moved Colburn towards the mass production of fashionable fiction. His production of (characteristically) three-deckers rose meteorically: 1823/1; 1824/4; 1825/6; 1826/14; 1827/18; 1828/30; 1829/39.

---

[129] See John Sutherland, 'The British Book Trade and the Crash of 1826', *The Library* (Sept. 1987), pp. 148–161.

DISRAELI

If there is one writer who can claim to be the brightest luminary in Henry Colburn's publishing career, it is a future Prime Minister. One of the greatest premiers in nineteenth-century British politics, most would concede. Benjamin Disraeli published his works with Colburn for a quarter of a century and established once and for all that Colburn succeeded not merely through advertising tricks or sleight of hand but through business acumen and personal attention to detail. Disraeli also proved, unwittingly, that he and Colburn were two of a kind.

Disraeli from the first had the highest expectations for himself as a novelist—and limitless aspirations for himself personally. In May 1824, while working in the city, he sent John Murray his first manuscript novel: *Aylmer Papillon,* a satire on England. Murray offered no reply, possibly because he did not want to hurt the young man's feelings. After a month's impatient waiting, Disraeli high-handedly instructed the publisher to burn it—as, notoriously, Murray had incinerated Byron's memoirs. The intimation was, clearly, that Disraeli was on a par with the author of *Don Juan.* Fragments of this early novel would resurface four years later in another book with a preposterous title, *The Voyage of Captain Popanilla;* this book, however, would not be published by Murray but by Henry Colburn.[130]

---

[130] Constructed around a *voyage imaginaire* to the South Seas, the story is a satire on utilitarianism—a political theory Disraeli had no time for.

By 1825, Benjamin Disraeli—not yet twenty-one years old—was feeling intolerably frustrated with his lot in life. He was strikingly clever and well educated, but as he had been taught at home and in small private schools, he had none of the social advantages that came with having attended public school or university. The one 'network' he had, his Jewish heritage (his surname means 'man of Israel'), isolated him further, although his agnostic father had taken the precaution of having Benjamin baptized into the Church of England.

The D'Israeli family were comfortably well off, but not rich. Not that riches would have helped Benjamin's political career in the early century had he remained true to his birth faith: the country did not have its first Jewish MP until Lionel de Rothschild in 1850. Even then, Queen Victoria opposed his being raised to the peerage since his wealth had come from a species of gambling. That is, banking.

Benjamin's father Isaac was a much-liked literary man, a lover of antiquarian 'curiosities' who preferred the scholarly seclusion of his library to the hubbub of fashionable society or the literary world of London. Isaac had arranged for Benjamin to read law with the most prominent Jewish barrister in the country, but his son was not interested—a fact that Benjamin advertised by turning up for his first day in chambers carrying, flamboyantly, a copy not of Blackstone's guide to the law but Spenser's *Faerie Queene*.

A legal career was quickly put aside, but Benjamin remained unsure about where his future lay. Fairyland perhaps. Of his talents he was quite sure, and the need for an income of his own was equally certain. Restless to do something and excited by the political and economic events of the day, he turned again to his father Isaac's closest contact in the book trade: his publisher, John Murray.

This was as good an indicator as any of Disraeli's aspirations: Murray, of course, had been Byron's publisher and was a dynastic presence in the London book trade. Some would say its leading literary presence. He was also proprietor of the 'heavy' Tory journal (with Scott as a star contributor) the *Quarterly Review*. Benjamin Disraeli approached Murray with a variety of schemes, including the creation of a new pro-Tory newspaper, the distribution of Tory pamphlets written by himself (a nobody), and investment in South American mining companies. He had never visited the Americas.

The normally cautious Murray was won over by Disraeli's bounding enthusiasm and self-confidence—a foretaste of the young man's future power as a political speaker. Birds in the trees were never safe when Disraeli was talking. This was the man who, thirty years later, would talk the Tory party out of being Tory and take what Carlyle called the great leap in the dark (the Second Reform Bill). But all this was yet to come. The schemes he proposed to Murray in 1825 were hare-brained. And guaranteed to be loss-making.

Indeed, when they had run their course and the sums were totted up, Murray felt duped and foolish. Financing Disraeli's proposals had cost both men heavily. A furious Murray severed ties with the entire D'Israeli family. On his part, Isaac vowed never to publish with the house of Murray or enter the firm's Albemarle Street door again. Benjamin's mother Maria made the eminently sensible comment that the publisher should have had more sense than to throw money at a callow twenty-year-old.[131] She knew her son better.

He recoiled into a depression, living in social seclusion with his family in Bloomsbury Square. Such breakdowns would happen regularly in his early life. The family holidayed, recuperating from the Murray storm, in Hyde House, near Amersham, rented from their friend Robert Plumer Ward. His novel *Tremaine* was currently the talk of the town—and, although the identity of the author remained a secret to the general public, the D'Israelis were in the know. Benjamin Disraeli was clearly thoughtful

---

[131] Jane Ridley, *The Young Disraeli*, p. 48.

about how a thousand pounds could be made so easily.[132] He saw a chance for himself. He too would write a silver-fork novel and make pots of money.

Disraeli confidently assumed that it was of no importance that he had not the slightest experience of fashionable life or its denizens. He would base his tale about a 'man of fashion' on what he had read, heard, and fantasised about wildly. The hero would be a grandiose version of Benjamin Disraeli. In this approach, the author was not mistaken: it was precisely what several other successful silver-fork novelists did. The novel Disraeli eventually concocted, *Vivian Grey*, had little plot but considerably more wit and 'dash' than the genre usually offered. And this debut novel indicates his interest in things political, and how a young man might rise in the political world.

Having completed the first few chapters, he showed them, confidentially, to Sara Austen—a confidant of Ward's who had laboriously copied out *Tremaine* (by hand!) so as to protect the writer's identity. Sara reacted to Disraeli's approach with friendly enthusiasm and set about arranging the novel's anonymous publication, for which, as with *Tremaine*, she turned (where else?) to New Burlington Street. She seems to have insinuated to Colburn that, like Ward's novel, the author of *Vivian Grey* was a prominent, and universally known, member of high society. Someone in the very upper swim.

Colburn saw through Austen's flummery, though. He offered only £200 for the copyright—his standard sum for a promising unknown but fully half of what he had offered for *Tremaine* and for Thomas Henry Lister's *Granby*. Colburn, now in his forties, had dealt with genuine aristocrats for twenty years and could smell the real thing. Disraeli was perfectly happy with the £200 ('down') and

---

[132] Subtitled 'Or the Man of Refinement', Ward's novel is a manual of manly, post-Byronic, style and formative in the establishment of the 'fashionable novel'.

publication got underway, with Sara Austen (as Disraeli's factotum) complaining bitterly to Colburn that his printers, Samuel and Richard Bentley, were slow and inefficient. Colburn took no notice and devoted his energies (and considerable money) to promoting the new novel.

Colburn's handling of the publicity for *Vivian Grey* demonstrates, in their fullest form, the techniques that had brought him commercial success while provoking, for their outrageousness, the fury of his competitors, who vengefully set out to destroy what professional reputation Henry Colburn had left. He used his 'interest' in the various periodicals owned or part-owned by him to circulate as 'literary intelligence' puffs about the real people, 'notables' all of them, who could expect to be caricatured in the daring new novel by an unknown hand. Colburn also demanded from William Jerdan a favourable notice in the *Literary Gazette*. There duly appeared, on publication, a three-page puff with extensive quotations.

Even at this stage, with publication underway, Colburn himself might not have known his author's name, as Disraeli was still hiding behind Sara Austen's skirts. At any rate, he certainly made great play with the author's anonymity, stirring up talk throughout London about the mysterious author of *Vivian Grey*. Speculation as to the author's identity intensified sensationally and demand for the book from circulating libraries, booksellers, and individual readers grew. Sales were gratifyingly brisk from the day of publication, 22 April 1826, onwards. In his excitement, Colburn seems to have gotten rather carried away with himself, telling the sub-editor of the *New Monthly* that 'I have a capital book out, *Vivian Grey*, the authorship is a great secret—a man of high fashion—very high—keeps the first society'.[133]

High fashion? If Colburn actually believed this (and the likelihood is that he didn't), then he must have been

---

[133] Redding, *Fifty Years' Recollections*, p 322.

as shocked as everybody else when the author's true identity finally emerged. As Jane Ridley, biographer of the young Disraeli, puts it, 'reviewers kicked themselves for swallowing Colburn's puff and allowing a young unknown Jew to pull the wool over their eyes'.[134] *The Literary Magnet* was sure that Disraeli and Sara Austen 'had conspired to defraud Colburn', while other magazines denounced both author and publisher for their hoax on the British public. Colburn handled the backlash to *Vivian Grey* with his typical serenity and keen business sense: he offered Disraeli £500 for a sequel. Doubtless with a smile on his face.

It is worth considering for a moment the reaction of Colburn's target audience to this widely publicised instance of puffery. While voices within the book trade lamented the terrible deception, readers were evidently untroubled by it: sales of *Vivian Grey* remained brisk. Indeed, Colburn would need to print a second edition that same year. High-minded critics tended to forget (or overlook) the fact that Henry Colburn's brand of literature was decidedly *light*— and the hyperbolic advertising and the authors' flights of fancy were part of the entertainment.

As Frances Wilson has usefully recognized, instead of vilifying the unfashionable author,

> readers accepted his pretence, and the novel was extremely popular, even after the author's true identity and social position was revealed. Indeed, the history of *Vivian Grey*…suggests that some readers may have recognized the authorial self-fashioning and claims to expertise on the ton as false or exaggerated but nevertheless accepted it, drawn to the novels by the potential pleasures of indulgence in the fashionable world or opportunity to mock the *ton*.[135]

---

[134] Op cit., 49.

[135] Wilson, op cit., 90–91.

The sales figures prove that puffery was not nearly as scandalous to Colburn's readers as it was to his critics and competitors; if it had been, he would have had to change his tactics to prevent outraged customers from going elsewhere.

Disraeli played up to his readers' love of sensation by cultivating a flamboyant personal style—one that stood out even in those days when dandyism was the fashion. As we have seen, the idea (or the dream) of being the new Byron had been with Disraeli at least since 1824. Not a poet himself, Disraeli channeled his Byronism into lacey shirts, lush, dark curls, rings on his fingers and bows on his shoes. Daniel Maclise's portrait of him from this time period (c.1826) ensured that a wider audience would see Disraeli in his overblown splendor. He would eventually extend his Byron worship to writing about him (in *Venetia*, 1837) and even recruiting his old servant, Tita, but image counted most heavily with Disraeli. If he could not fit in with the ton, he could outdo them. It was just the approach Henry Colburn took with so-called gentleman publishers.

Despite Disraeli's genuine gifts for cultivating public appeal, the young author was far more sensitive to criticism than Colburn ever was and initially felt hurt by the row over *Vivian Grey*. He was disparaged as everything from a puppy to a near-criminal fraud—and, of course, a Jew. Anti-Semitic abuse would greet him at every turn, no matter how high he rose in society, and it started early. The onslaught may have precipitated the depressive illness he suffered in the summer of 1826, which was only alleviated by a tour of the continent with the faithful Sara Austen and her husband Benjamin. First-class travel abroad was always Disraeli's sovereign remedy for whatever ailed or depressed him. On his return to London, the author—revived but still burdened with debt—gratefully accepted Colburn's generous offer for a sequel and duly delivered *Vivian Grey, Part II*.

Published on 23 February 1827, the sequel did not sell as well as the original nor is it, in literary terms, as good as its predecessor. Disraeli responded to the criticism by writing an article for Colburn's *New Monthly Magazine* that explained, brazenly, the classical precedents for some of its scenes. It was not fashionable fiction: it was high literature. The publisher passed Disraeli's piece on to the editor, Thomas Campbell, who proved less pliable than his counterpart at the *Literary Gazette*. He refused to include Disraeli's defence without extensive revisions, telling the publisher (his employer) in the haughtiest terms: 'The article you propose to insert is a puff of the most extravagant and iniquitous praise such as I could not shew my face in society if it suffered to appear under my auspices'.[136]

When Colburn pressed him on the matter, the ostentatiously high-minded Campbell wrote a reply dated 26 March 1827 (while pocketing the generous monthly stipend for which he did so little), saying: 'there never was greater infatuation than your forgetting how much higher you stand as the proprietor of an unimpeachable & honourable work like the New Monthly than as the proprietor of a gossiping & ephemeral novel'.[137] 'Infatuation' is a curious choice of words to describe Colburn's attitude towards the author of *Vivian Grey*, but Campbell won this little battle. Colburn, for once, backed down. At this point, he could not afford to lose the poet-editor, even for Benjamin Disraeli.

Perhaps it was Colburn's personal fondness for Disraeli that prompted him to offer the young man another £500 for his next novel, sight unseen, whilst entreating him to write, at will, for his portfolio of periodicals. In a sense, he adopted the young author. But Colburn also had sound business reasons for his open-handedness. The

---

[136] Hughenden Papers, 235/3, 10–11.

[137] National Art Library, F.48.E.11, 60–61.

William Maginn

"THE DOCTOR"

generous sum he disbursed was calculated to forge a long future connection, binding Disraeli to him with debts of gratitude. He would be a client author—like Lady Morgan or (for as long as he could put up with Colburn) Bulwer.

Colburn's shrewd professional judgement was that Disraeli's future productions for New Burlington Street would prove as successful as his first had done. Which, on the whole, they were. He was a rising man. Colburn also wanted Disraeli to write at top speed, before the éclat of *Vivian Grey*, the way it had excited the fiction-reading public, faded. Puffery was a short-lived thing. Colburn's decision to indenture Disraeli provoked the usual spiteful wrath from his rivals, who saw it (wrongly, as usual) as an infringement of authorial independence; a hobbling of genius. When William Maginn satirized Colburn in *Whitehall: Or the Days of George IV* (1827), he aimed squarely at Colburn's mass production of popular novels. Maginn's burlesque is not badly done and, for what it reveals about the trade's perception of Colburn, merits a small digression.

'Henri Le Grand' ('Henry the Great'), also known as 'Harry Badger' (i.e., 'bully'—one who badgers) and 'The Master', is a literary slave driver. He owns a manufactory on Burlington Street as crammed with hacks as a Lancashire cotton mill is with machine-handlers, 'fifteen to a desk', whom he refers to as 'journeymen'—day labourers. He drives his workers mercilessly, complaining, for example, that 'there's not a man among you who has done a sheet, this blessed day, yet'.[138] A 'sheet' is sixteen octavo pages and it is not yet nine o'clock in the morning. Quantity is all. The Master's foreman weighs, rather than reads manuscripts as they roll off the novel-writing assembly line. The Master turns on one luckless youth and shouts:

---

[138] Maginn 306.

'You, Sir! you passed me off, as materials fit for high life,
a commodity that belonged to a Jew washer-woman.
Dang me, but I could find it in my heart to let them
there confounded slinking shoulders feel the taste of
the whip!'[139]

The Master's verbal assault is only stopped when the
young author faints from fear, gashing his head on the
fine marble floor—paid for with the labour of such as him.

The 'Jew washer-woman' insult makes clear that the
young writer is a caricature of Disraeli. There was only one
famous Jewish novelist in England. The Master's crude
remark, of course, alludes specifically to his firm's publicity
surrounding *Vivian Grey*. 'Dr. Maginn' (he was hugely
proud of his university classics education) also takes a swipe
at Colburn's presumed social origins (that 'guttersnipe'
again) by having Henri Le Grand, in contradiction to
his name, speak like an uncouth oaf. Henry Colburn, of
course, was nothing of the sort; it was his methods that
were 'ungentlemanly'.

The scene in the literary factory continues as, turning to
the bleeding Disraeli (as we assume),

> The Master displayed, however, a touch of a feeling mind
> upon this occasion, for though he was obliged to keep his
> workmen in order, he was naturally of a kind disposition.
>
> 'Get him to bed', said he, 'and put some horse turpentine
> in the cut, and you may give him some beef-tea with his
> gruel. You need not come to-morrow to work, my lad.'
>
> The grateful looks of the youth as he was borne out
> testified his sense of the clemency of his master, and
> impressed Smithers [the hero of *Whitehall*] with a high
> opinion of the manner in which affairs were carried on
> in the manufactory.[140]

---

[139] Ibid. 307–308.

[140] Ibid. 308–309.

The lampoon is funny in its way, but grossly unfair in every other way. Whatever other criticisms could be brought against Colburn, he was provably generous to the authors who, like Disraeli, were loyal to him. 'His' authors. He gave them much better fare than gruel. Maginn nonetheless makes his points about the 'manufacturing' of literature and the way that Colburn had, in a sense, 'taken possession' of the young Disraeli. And Maginn was by no means the only person in Literary London who was talking about it.

Disraeli—in need of cash at this and, indeed, every stage of his career—gladly accepted Colburn's offer of £500 for a new novel to follow the two *Vivian Greys*. Money he had lost in the John Murray affair was still owed and a political career remained out of reach. Accordingly, after another bout of nervous illness, he turned out the one-volume satire called *The Voyage of Captain Popanilla*. Colburn published the unimpressive thing, in June 1828, as by 'the author of *Vivian Grey*'. Shortly thereafter, Disraeli became ill yet again.

His biographers believe Disraeli's health problems at this stage of his life were caused by depression—or 'melancholy', as the nineteenth century called it—a condition from which his father Isaac chronically suffered. Who knows? Whatever the cause, Benjamin fell back on his own favourite remedy: international travel. This time, he would take a journey to the Levant—the Jewish homeland. It would not be the cheapest of medicines. And duns were circling round him. His only current source of income (other than loans from trusting friends) were the handful of articles he submitted to Colburn's *Court Journal*.

Ultimately, there was only one means of acquiring money enough for his ambitious trip to the other side of the world. On 8 December 1829, he explained it, with disarming frankness, to Benjamin Austen:

> I fear I must *hack* for it. A literary prostitute I have never yet been, tho' born in an age of general prostitution, and tho' I have more than once been subject to temptations

which might have been the *ruination* of a less virtuous young woman. My muse however is still a virgin, but the mystical flower, I fear, must soon be plucked. Colburn I suppose will be the bawd. Tempting Mother Colburn![141]

The bitter jests about literary prostitution and the depiction of his publisher as his 'bawd' are illuminating (as, in an odd way, is the transposition of Disraeli and Colburn into feminine roles), but Disraeli does not create the impression that these things kept him awake at night. One perceives that, when needs must, he had no real misgivings about 'hacking': whether in journalism or fiction. Nor was he overly concerned that the sole source of the money he needed was Henry Colburn. Outside of his dark spells of melancholy, Disraeli rarely lacked confidence and, despite being half his publisher's age, he believed he could hold his own with Mother Colburn.

Disraeli duly turned to work on the novel that would emerge as *The Young Duke*—a novel as silver-fork as its title promised. About half-way through writing, on 14 February 1830, he lifted his pen to consult with his publisher about the work in progress. The letter reveals so much about the Colburn-Disraeli relationship that it merits quoting in full:

PRIVATE

Dear Sir,

Forward the enclosed [letter to Catherine Gore] and don't look pale about the postage, which I will religiously discharge when we meet. I have not forgotten you, tho' the preparations for my departure and another cause have prevented me lately sending you a contribution. In a word, being declared to be in a decline, which is all

---

[141] Disraeli, *Letters*, 1, 74.

stuff, but really with positive Exile, probable Death, and possible Damnation hanging over me, I have been fool enough to be intent upon a novel—But such a novel! It will astound you, draw tears from Princesses, and grins from Printers devils: it will atone for all the stupid books you have been lately publishing, and allow me to die in a blaze. In a word to give you an idea of it. It is exactly the kind of work which you wo[ul]d write yourself, if you had time, and delightfully adapted to the most corrupt taste. This immortal work which will set all Europe afire and not be forgotten till at least 3 months has only one fault—it is not written.

Seriously however *a volume and ½* are finished, but as I must go off before the end of March I am afraid it is impossible to let you have it, but perhaps I can finish it at Rome before I go off to Greece, and then you can have it for next Season. A pity because it is exactly suited to the present. Write if you wish me to hatch this Phoenix—but any rate be SECRET AS THE GRAVE.

In haste

B. Disraeli

P.S. I have not yet read Mrs. C[atherine] G[ore]'s novel, which how[eve]r, I have. You are publishing a good deal of dull stuff. *Imitations of imitations.*[142]

If ever proof were needed of Henry Colburn's fondness for Benjamin Disraeli—his 'infatuation', in Campbell's words—this letter is it. Colburn was largely inured to jibes about his publications and privately seems to have had few illusions about the literary quality of many of them, but it is difficult to imagine *any* publisher allowing an author on

---

[142] Disraeli, *Letters,* 1, 74.

his own payroll to derogate the 'dull' and 'stupid' books he was producing. And if such remarks were unimaginable from a seasoned author, how much more from a very young author whose last two efforts were still languishing in the warehouse. Nonetheless, Disraeli clearly sensed that he was on safe ground here and trusted that Colburn would find his outrageousness endearing. Which, it seems, Colburn did.

Not least among Disraeli's charms was his obvious ability to discern precisely the kind of novel which suited New Burlington Street. It had to be a work of the moment, not expected to last more than a season, if as long as that, and predictably similar to the genre pattern set by earlier writers (such as Catherine Gore). It must be a 'light' novel which delivered laughter and tears and a hint of 'real life' scandal. Real 'high' life, that is. Readers of silver-fork fiction wanted, insatiably, more of the same. So sure was Disraeli of the Colburnian product required that he could fantasise about the novel Colburn himself would have written, if he had time—a subtly flattering idea to float to one's publisher.

But there is more to this letter than proof of Colburn's elastic tolerance and deep affection for Disraeli. The whole thing is written in such a familiar and facetious tone that one can easily lose sight of the fact that it is actually a *business* letter, from an author offering a new work to his publisher. Incredibly, it even mocks the business they are in. Considering that four short years earlier, Disraeli would only approach Colburn through a third party, it is extraordinary that he should now feel able to write him such a casual and personal letter. But, then, it is essentially a silver-fork letter. Brimming with flair and confidence, walking a fine line between humour and scandal, showing off Disraeli's easy way with words—as writing samples go, it isn't a bad one at all.

What goes unsaid in this and in Disraeli's other letters is important, too. He had quickly discerned how Colburn puffed novels and how the press would react to anything with Colburn's imprint on it. Though he had been hurt by the vicious reaction that had met *Vivian Grey*, his first major appearance on the literary stage, there is no evidence that he disapproved of Colburn's puffing techniques. On the contrary, as someone who was almost as eager to sell books as Colburn was, Disraeli could readily appreciate the benefits of such creative marketing. A man who would later steal the Liberals' clothes, changing England in the process, Disraeli was not overly scrupulous himself. Indeed, having agreed verbally to give Colburn *The Young Duke* upon its completion, and taken money for it, he then turned around and secretly offered it to Murray. Having already been burned by Disraeli's earlier schemes, though, Murray wanted nothing to do with it and ended the author's Byronic aspirations for good. Disraeli went right back to Colburn to seal the deal and then headed for the Levant with another £500 payment in his purse. His English debts could be paid off later.

Between Colburn's receiving the manuscript of *The Young Duke* in May 1830 and its publication in April 1831, there was a strange pause. No definite explanation for the delay has been discovered. It seems, from other evidence, not to have been any breakdown in relations (or indignation about the Murray business). An initial delay in *The Young Duke's* publication is explained by the letter of 14 February 1830 in which Disraeli says the novel must be held back until the next 'season', which began in October. The ensuing delay might be explained by the wave of populist sentiment after the death of George IV, making it an unpropitious time to publish the dandiacal story of a fabulously wealthy aristocrat. This, at least, was how Benjamin Disraeli's sister Sarah saw it, making the sardonic comment: 'in this our mobbing and huzzaing age, Colburn deems us too vulgar'.[143]

---

[143] Ridley, op cit., 80.

When it was finally published, *The Young Duke* actually lived up to the claims its author had made for it, offering all the glitter and an even better story than its predecessors. It follows the career of a young man ('youth' was always Disraeli's great theme, climaxing with his 'Young England' political movement) who comes to learn, after predictable trials, that the love of a good woman is more valuable than his money and property. It's a conventionally sentimental conclusion, particularly pleasing to women readers, but on the way to this banal happily-ever-after it introduces an entertaining profusion of silver-forkery. One of Disraeli's characters even quotes a recipe for this sort of literary production: 'Take a pair of pistols and a pack of cards, a cookery-book and a set of new quadrilles; mix them up with half an intrigue and a whole marriage, and divide them into three equal portions.'[144]

The Young Duke continues in this humorously self-mocking vein (like the letter that preceded it) while beginning to craft the author's trademark 'Dizzy' image on a level beyond the flashy outfits. The political Benjamin Disraeli would sound not unlike one of his own characters from the silver-fork universe: 'I never venture to a strange dinner, lest I should stumble upon a fashionable novelist; and even with all this vigilance, and all this denial, I have an intimate friend whom I cannot cut, and who, they say, writes for the *Court Journal*.'[145]

In the novel, the *Court Journal* writer turns out to be our hero's brother; in reality, it was, of course, our hero himself. Disraeli went even further toward blurring the distinction between fiction and reality by introducing Ward and Bulwer into *The Young Duke* by name. If Colburn had not already been entranced by Disraeli's fashionability and facetiousness, he must surely have chortled at his adoption of the Colburnian 'method'. Disraeli made outrageous self-promotion stylish.

---

[144] *The Young Duke*, 3 vols (1831), III, 122.

[145] *The Young Duke*, III, 162.

In his previous dealings with Henry Colburn, up to the time of *The Young Duke*, Disraeli had bypassed any editorial staff and dealt directly with the publisher himself. But on his return with the Austens from the Levant, he was destined to find things much changed at New Burlington Street. A new co-manager had joined the firm. In September 1829, Colburn had taken on one of his printers, Richard Bentley, as an equal partner for a three-year period. Henceforth it was 'Colburn and Bentley' that Disraeli would have to deal with.

The partnership, which would prove momentous for both men, will be examined below, but the salient point for Disraeli at this stage of his career was that Colburn intended to go into semi-retirement in 1832, leaving the commissioning and publishing of new books entirely in Bentley's hands. Disraeli would be part and parcel of the commercial 'good will' Colburn was passing on to Bentley. Colburn was moving on and out of the business. He would, on becoming a free agent, continue to manage his periodicals and 'work', as the term was, his large store of old copyrights as and when he saw fit.

Bentley would, in the event, prove a disastrously bad choice as partner and successor. The men's personalities were too different. Though younger than Colburn by a good ten years, Bentley was in character more sober, methodical, and conventional. He singularly lacked 'flair'. And in contrast to Colburn's good-humoured and relaxed approach to business matters, Bentley proved to be a legalistic bean counter, always looking at the petty cash box. Colburn despised anything 'petty'.

Things went awry from the very beginning. It was a publishing marriage made in Hell. Bentley was frightened by the vast (as he thought) sums Colburn was routinely shelling out to favoured authors. The 'trade' was still reeling from the 1826 'catastrophe'—horns, everywhere other than New Burlington Street, had been pulled in. Bentley was appalled by the expense and, possibly, moral dubiousness, of his partner's habitual puffery. Colburn, for his part, was annoyed at what he saw as Bentley's meddling in his perfectly successful business practices and the small-mindedness of his partner's treatment of what were now 'their' authors.

Bentley manifested none of the warmth, tolerance, or understanding that marked Colburn's easy-going relationships with most of his writers and the literary world generally. It was not at all in Bentley's personality to be easy-going. It was all very hard-going for him. Richard Bentley could never have cultivated and nurtured the young Disraeli, for example, in the way Colburn had so successfully done. And it was on record that Disraeli (or at least Sara Austen) was unimpressed with how slowly Bentley had printed *Vivian Grey*. Nor, one deduces, did Disraeli like Bentley's manners, now that the other man was his co-publisher. He, of course, put up with whatever grievance he may have felt. As always with him, 'needs must'. He needed, bluntly, money. First-class travel expenses had not improved his financial position. Thrift was not one of his virtues.

Disraeli confided to friends that Colburn had intimated he was willing to help fund his travels privately, off the partnership books, writing in a letter, on 3 November 1831 that Colburn 'had promised to honour my draught to any discreet amount'.[146] Discreet was an elastic term in Disraeli's vocabulary.

By his usual desperate remedies, Disraeli managed on this occasion to circumvent the need for any personal loan from Colburn. Nevertheless, his frequent references to such offers by Colburn reveal how much this degree of trust flattered his ego. In stark contrast to the Colburn way of doing things is a letter to Disraeli dated just one month later, 9 December 1831.[147] The letter is, on this occasion,

---

[146] Disraeli, *Letters*, 120.

[147] British Library, Add.MS.46640, 71.

from Colburn and Bentley. It reminds him that he had received a £100 advance on a second edition of *The Young Duke,* but since a second edition had not yet been called for, the firm wanted its money back. It is impossible to reconcile this note with the earlier letter and with Colburn's usual financial liberality—why would he demand the return of £100 from Disraeli only weeks after offering him a virtually unlimited sum? Bentley was clearly behind this pettiness. Colburn, one can confidently assume, was not worried about getting small sums back. It was beneath him. And although the letter is formally signed with both partners' names, it is wholly in the handwriting of Richard Bentley.

The Bentley problem, so to call it, surfaced elsewhere in connection with Colburn's periodicals, which had taken on new importance for him as the main supporting prop of his imminent semi-retirement. After the poet Thomas Campbell resigned as editor of Colburn's flagship journal, the *New Monthly,* in 1830, the publisher assumed his editorial duties until he could find another literary celebrity to take the post. In a typically shrewd interweaving of business concerns, Colburn hired his own silver-fork novelist, Edward Lytton Bulwer.

Though dismissed by *Fraser's* as a 'silver-fork polisher', Bulwer had a genuine patrician pedigree.[148] His first novel, *Falkland* (1827), was a failure, but Colburn accepted the manuscript for his second novel, *Pelham* (1828), and handed it to his in-house readers. When Shoberl advised against it and Ollier contradicted him, Colburn read it himself and declared that it would be the book of the year. It was. Read as a satire by some and as a pure fashionable novel by others, *Pelham* enjoyed strong sales not just in 1828 but throughout the nineteenth century. Bulwer followed

---

[148] Quoted in Sadleir, *Bulwer,* 258. Over the years, he would be known as Bulwer, Lytton, Bulwer-Lytton (with and without the hyphen), and Baron Lytton of Knebworth. In these early days with Colburn, however, he was still just plain old Bulwer.

it up with other successful titles for Colburn, but it was *Pelham* that made his name—and that prompted Benjamin Disraeli to write him what was essentially a fan letter. It was a tentative start to a strong and lasting friendship between two of Colburn's most illustrious authors.

Bulwer became a close friend of Colburn's as well, and they had corresponded, warmly, while Disraeli was away on his travels. On his return, Disraeli found that editor and publisher had been arranging to move him from his spot in the relatively minor *Court Journal,* to whose pages he had been a regular contributor, to the higher profile *New Monthly.* Bulwer informed Disraeli of the fact in a letter of 8 November 1831:

My dear Disraeli

Pray let me not be the last—if I have not been among the first to congratulate you on your safe return. I only heard of it yesterday from our mutual Ally of the Burlington Street Delphos 'Mr. Disraeli, Sir, is come to town young Mr. Disraeli! Won't he give us a nice light article about his travels?'…Of that hereafter. But while, at present neglecting the hint of our worthy Publisher, I by no means forget it.[149]

This is a jocular letter, but it has serious undertones: if 'the Burlington Street Delphos' is Colburn and Bentley, and their 'mutual Ally' within it is Colburn, then the enemy they are allied against is, logically, Richard Bentley. Bulwer's distaste for Colburn's partner never quite matched Disraeli's, but two years into the Colburn and Bentley alliance, he clearly still considered only the former to be his 'worthy Publisher'. It's a telling letter.

Colburn, for his part, was still open-handed with 'his' authors, as he continued to see them. After he and Bulwer

---

[149] Hughenden Papers, 104/1, 21–22.

had coaxed Disraeli into writing three articles for the *New Monthly* (presumably with little difficulty), Bulwer wrote in his editorial capacity to Disraeli on 18 August 1832 to inform him that 'Mr Colburn has sent me [9 pounds, 9 shillings] for your little paper [...] being at the rate of 20 [guineas] a sheet—His very highest Reward'.[150] Highest reward would have rung very happily in Disraeli's ears.

At the dissolution of their partnership on 31 August 1832, Colburn and Bentley were no longer on civil speaking terms with each other. Colburn had retreated to his counting house on Great Marlborough Street and had started to wonder about the wisdom of selling his 'good will'—a cruel misnomer—to Bentley. On his side, the former printer had problems of his own. On becoming head of the New Burlington Street firm, Bentley had confidently expected to become the 'master' (as Maginn would have called it) of the still highly profitable silver-fork genre. But because Colburn had taken the lucrative pre-1829 back-catalogue with him, the earliest (and some of the best) silver-fork titles were outside of Bentley's control. They were Colburn's property. Even worse, many of the genre's luminaries, including Mrs. Gore and Lady Bury, had left with Colburn. He was their man. Privately they had probably liked Bentley's manners no more than Disraeli.

Bentley was affronted. Could these authors not see, as he so clearly saw, what Colburn was? Colburn, however, was now reaping the reward of years of treating his authors pastorally, indulgently and, above all, generously. It was no surprise that they preferred doing business with him. They liked him. Though the partnership's deed of dissolution decreed that Colburn should no longer publish new works, some of his loyal authors made a point of declining to publish with Bentley either. Most continued to contribute to Colburn's magazines, as they long had in the

---

[150] Hughenden Papers, 104/1, 34.

past. To Bentley's dismay, Benjamin Disraeli was firmly with this majority. He, too, was a Colburn man. Bentley had inherited a crown without jewels.

The Colburn and Bentley split hit Disraeli almost as hard as it hit the two erstwhile partners. At the time of *The Young Duke*, Disraeli had happily contracted for a new novel, thinking only of Henry Colburn as his publisher, much as Bulwer had. As the partnership's dissolution approached, however, Disraeli foresaw that he would now be unhappily contracted to Richard Bentley. Solely. Feeling the need to escape this obligation—and recognizing an opportunity to move on to a more prestigious publisher—Disraeli wrote again with his usual mix of servility and self-confidence to John Murray. In a letter dated 4 March 1832, Disraeli explained that 'in quitting my present publisher, I incur, from the terms of our last agreement, a virtual penalty, which I have no means to pay except by the proceeds of my pen'.

Disraeli accompanied this with a flagrant demand for an advance on unwritten work to pay the penalty.[151] Always susceptible to Disraeli's self-promoting enthusiasm, Murray agreed to the deal. It was a mistake. Disraeli soon found out what Colburn had known all along: namely that top-tier literary publishers such as Murray, Longman and Blackwood, did not know how to promote fashionable novels or have a suitable clientele for them. When Murray published Disraeli's subsequent novel *Contarini Fleming* at the end of 1832, it was an utter failure, despite loyal (mendacious) endorsement from Colburn's *Literary Gazette* and *New Monthly Magazine,* the latter still under Bulwer's editorial management. Murray, his fingers burned, declined to publish Disraeli's next offering, *The Wondrous Tale of Alroy*. Saunders and Otley, Colburn's successors when he sold his circulating library, published the feeble work in 1833. Disraeli got on well with these partners and

---

[151] Disraeli, *Letters*, p. 148.

enthused about the support and encouragement they gave him. But the honeymoon with 'S and O', as Disraeli called them, was short-lived. When the partners registered their displeasure with a political satire Disraeli was preparing with his sister Sarah, *A Year at Hartlebury, or the Election,* he wrote to her that 'I am in the greatest rage with S and O'.[152] They went on to publish the book in 1834 but, as they had no success with either it nor *Alroy,* they like Murray politely declined any further fiction from Disraeli's pen. He had priced himself out of their market.

Adding to Disraeli's woes at this point were the numerous parliamentary election campaigns he mounted and lost (two in 1832 and a further two in 1835). Through all the difficulties and trials, however, he continued to receive moral and, more importantly, financial support from Colburn, who now hired him as a regular, salaried, contributor to his *New Monthly.* After signing a contract on this matter in May 1834, it is probably not wholly coincidental that Disraeli complimented Colburn, writing, 'I think your Mag: is improving'.[153] Improving with the addition of Benjamin Disraeli, that was. Nonetheless, despite Colburn's assistance, Disraeli was still having difficulty ordering his financial affairs as late as 1836. (Ridley wittily calls him 'a debtor by profession' at this stage in his life.[154]) He owed Benjamin Austen money and needed an advance from Colburn to cover that obligation. The publisher was apparently not quick enough off the mark with an ex gratia £100. Disraeli wrote, unapologetically, to Austen about the unconscionable delay on Colburn's part, adding 'you know what a difficult man he is to manage'. Significantly, though, Disraeli immediately goes on to qualify this by explaining, 'At this moment too he is entirely absorbed with a new arrangement of his Magazine

---

[152] Disraeli, *Letters,* p. 306.

[153] Disraeli, *Letters,* p. 333.

[154] Ridley, op cit., 189.

and the quarrels of rival editors [Theodore Hook and S. C. Hall]'.[155]

The year 1836, however, marked a turning point for Henry Colburn and, by extension, for Benjamin Disraeli. Colburn's magazines and working of old copyrights were going fairly well, but he wanted to return to the front-line publishing of new works. He finally found a legal loophole that would let him do it. Bentley, loath to compete commercially and frightened of taking him to court, settled with his former partner for a hefty fee. Colburn thus returned to the trade he loved, settling his firm into his Great Marlborough Street premises. Disraeli evidently made some sort of gesture in support of Colburn at this momentous (for Colburn) point. In a letter to Disraeli dated 22 August 1836, Colburn wrote: 'I am exceedingly obliged to you for your advocacy of my cause; for I think you entertain a kindly feeling towards me'.[156]

After the instability that marked most of the post-Crash decade, for both Colburn and Disraeli, everything fell into place again over the course of 1836 and 1837: Colburn wholly re-established himself as a publisher of new works and Disraeli finally made it to Parliament, as Tory M.P. for Maidstone. He nevertheless found time to write the novel *Henrietta Temple*, for which Colburn paid him his highest fee yet.[157] Colburn published the novel on 1 December 1836 and set his revamped publicity machine in motion. It was in as good shape as ever. With *Henrietta Temple*, he produced Disraeli's biggest sale since *Vivian Grey*—a triumph for author and publisher alike.[158] A letter from Disraeli to his sister jubilated in the men's joint success:

---

[155] Disraeli, *Letters*, p. 523.

[156] Hughenden Papers, 235/3, 21–22.

[157] Disraeli, *Letters*, 511.

[158] Ridley, op cit., 183.

I saw Colburn yesterday who met me with a smiling face. The sale is very brisk and increases. [...] He is in excellent spirits and says if I can only manage to get out another book this season, of a deep and high interest, he thinks I shall have regained at a bound all the lost ground of the last 3 years in this sort of work. He has offered me 600£ for a novel by the 1st of May, and wishes it to be serious and pathetic.[159]

One hears the echo of Colburn's speech in that phrase 'serious and pathetic'.

Henrietta Temple demonstrated, incontrovertibly, that Colburn could succeed where more prestigious publishers like Murray had failed. It cemented his business relationship with Disraeli, permanently: even when he could take his fiction anywhere he wanted to. No longer an idealistic virgin in books, Disraeli had learnt to be content with his 'bawd'.

Disraeli embraced Colburn's plan to hurry out another novel in the following year but briefly lost his confidence in the new book. As he sat down to work on it, he quipped that he would be ruining Colburn.[160] It was Colburn's own confidence, however, that bolstered him and kept him going. Later the same month, Disraeli noted with gratification that 'He [Colburn] cannot receive too much of my writings now he says or too speedily'.[161] Not only was Colburn eager to return to publishing new works, he evidently was trying to make up for lost time. *Venetia* was duly published in May 1837, and though it was not an unqualified success as had been *Henrietta Temple*, the novel covered its costs.

Venetia was duly published, in three volumes, in May 1837. It is the last effusion of Disraeli romantic fiction and

---

[159] Disraeli, *Letters*, p. 543.

[160] Disraeli, *Letters*, 551.

[161] Disraeli, *Letters*, 567.

Byronic themes and his move towards political fiction. Marmion and Lady Annabel Herbert separate on account of his republican sympathies. He goes off to become a general in the American revolutionary army, and after the war resides in Italy—itself seething with republicanism. The Herberts' daughter Venetia grows up in England fascinated with her father, whom she knows by his portrait and by his vibrant poetry, and the redolence of her Italianate name.

Venetia's love affair with Lord Cadurcis is obstructed by her mother, who objects to the young man's radical politics. Venetia suffers a physical breakdown and goes to Italy to recuperate. There she effects a reconciliation between her parents. Cadurcis arrives and, in his turn, is reconciled to Lady Herbert. The story ends tragically, however, when Cadurcis (echoes of Shelley's death) is drowned in a squall in the Bay of Spezzia. Venetia subsequently marries Cadurcis's cousin, Captain George.

The relationship between Colburn and Disraeli was now firmer than ever. On 15 December, the new M.P. wrote to his sister about Talfourd's copyright bill, saying, 'I suggested a clause to Talfourd, with the idea of which I had been furnished by Colburn'.[162] What the clause was and whether it was eventually enshrined in law we do not know, but it testifies to Disraeli's faith in Colburn's judgment on all matters relating to the book trade and its legal regulation. Colburn must have been gratified to learn that he, a mere trade publisher who had just survived a bruising struggle with Bentley, had the ear of a rising young M.P. and had made a contribution to parliamentary debate. Little wonder he was smiling and 'in excellent spirits'.

---

[162] Disraeli, *Letters*, 690.

LOYALTY AND FRIENDSHIP

The story of Disraeli's relationship with Henry Colburn has been related at length because of the future prime minister's significance and because of what it reveals about the publisher—but not because it is the only insight we have into Colburn's relationships with his authors. Posterity has not been kind to Lady Caroline Lamb, James Boaden, and Thomas Henry Lister, but these minor novelists were major correspondents of Henry Colburn, and the primary collections of their letters, preserved in Britain's National Art Library, have much to tell us.

Lady Caroline Lamb's brief literary career was, even in her own lifetime, easily overshadowed by her affair with Lord Byron and its attendant controversy. This is hardly to be wondered at, in view of Byron's celebrity and Lady Caroline's dubious prose, but her works were of considerable importance to her and made a real impact on her family and on Colburn. He published *Glenarvon* in 1816 and *Graham Hamilton* in 1821, and though the correspondence also refers to other works, they do not appear to have been published by Colburn. As a barely veiled depiction of the Byron affair, *Glenarvon* went through three editions in its first year—a considerable coup for Colburn at that early stage of his career. *Graham Hamilton* seems to have enjoyed respectable sales, though we are dependent upon Lady Caroline for that assessment: 'I hope you are pleased about Graham for it is liked'.[163]

Her unstable temperament and sometimes bizarre behaviour is too complicated to be sketched out here, since even her biographers have had difficulty discerning precisely what she did and why. Crompton indicates the problem when he notes that 'her famous remark after meeting Byron—"mad, bad, and dangerous to know"— proved in this affair even more applicable to herself'.[164] Thus, once Lady Caroline and Henry Colburn struck a deal on *Glenarvon* (after Byron's publisher, John Murray, had predictably turned it down), the publication process became one of high drama. A natural intriguer, the author suggested to her publisher schemes to arouse interest in the novel's anonymity,[165] and then complained when her identity was found out. When one bookseller actually advertised *Glenarvon* under her name, she wrote to Colburn: 'I do entreat you to go instantly & have it stopped'.[166] She wasted a good deal of his time vacillating over whether she should attach her name to subsequent editions, but her husband William (subsequently Lord Melbourne) cut to the chase and asked Colburn not to publish any new editions at all.[167]

Throughout their correspondence Lady Caroline frequently lauded her publisher for 'your zeal your kindness & above all your good nature',[168] and it is interesting to see William Lamb adopt a similarly flattering tone in his letter to Colburn, remarking on 'your good sense & knowledge of the world as well as of your profession'. Colburn's good sense told him to keep Lady Caroline happy, which he

---

[163] National Art Library, F.48.E.22, 51–52.

[164] Crompton 197.

[165] National Art Library, F.48.E.22, 16–17.

[166] National Art Library, F.48.E.22, 32–33.

[167] National Art Library, F.48.E.22, 23–24.

[168] National Art Library, F.48.E.22, 11–13.

attempted to do by cheerfully meeting her many requests for complimentary copies for her friends and stocking her private library with complimentary copies of his other books, just as he would later do for Disraeli. Lady Caroline's letters are mostly undated but they are so arranged as to show a change from this pleasant but somewhat distant relationship to one more dependent upon personal visits. Thus, she began frequently to invite Colburn to her house, though certain letters make her invitations sound more like demands: 'I want you to come here could you call at 4 if by any accident I do not see you today, be home at 11 tomorrow'.[169] As preparations for the publication of Lady Caroline's *Graham Hamilton* progressed, Colburn obtained entry to the Lambs' country house: 'I believe I had better come to Town to see you unless you would like some sunday [*sic*] to come here to me. The expence is [illegible] I need not besides add how happy I shall be to defray it & to receive you, you can either sleep here or return the same day as is convenient I wish also to talk to you on many subjects'.[170]

This bonhomie led Lady Caroline to send Colburn occasional presents, including a brace of partridges,[171] and on one occasion to ask him to perform a very unusual and strangely intimate task. 'Would you kindly do me the favour', she wrote, 'to see this person whose address I inclose, to tell me sincerely whether you think she is a respectable & accomplished Governess [...] let me really know what you think of her'.[172] Colburn's response to this entreaty might have established just how far he was prepared to go to please his authors, but it has lamentably gone unrecorded.

The latter part of Colburn's relationship with Lady Caroline was marred by the advent of one Wilmington

---

[169] National Art Library, F.48.E.22, 75–76.

[170] National Art Library, F.48.E.22, 31.

[171] National Art Library, F.48.E.22, 46–47.

[172] National Art Library, F.48.E.22, 90–91.

Fleming, who seems to have been both con artist and blackmailer. He evidently contacted both author and publisher but the particulars of their intercourse have yet to be fully unravelled. Until they are, we have at least a glimpse of the trust that Colburn was able to establish with even his flightiest authors.

If not flighty, James Boaden brought his own set of problems and peculiarities to the table. Primarily a dramatist in his early life, he then took to writing biographies of theatrical people, and it was in this latter capacity that he attracted Colburn as his publisher. For him, Boaden produced the *Life of Mrs. Siddons* (1827) and the memoir attached to the *Private Correspondence of David Garrick with the Most Celebrated Persons of His Time* (1831), and perhaps other similar titles. He also wrote two novels, at least one of which—*The Man of Two Lives* (1828)—was published from 8 New Burlington Street (and lauded in the pages of Disraeli's *Venetia* for good measure). Boaden's correspondence makes plain that he was perennially short of funds and that he relied on Colburn, *as a friend,* to make up the shortfall.[173] Practically every letter to Colburn preserved in the National Art Library refers to these circumstances. For example, on 17 January 1826, Boaden requested £100 with the injunction, 'Pray don't fail me!'[174]; four months later he thanked Colburn for another £100[175]; even in his last letter, of 28 September 1829, he asked for £50 'on account of anything', concluding, 'My dear friend, you must not refuse me, seriously'.[176]

The naked honesty of Boaden's appeals to Colburn has a certain charm, but he must have wheedled a serious

---

[173] If the *Dictionary of National Biography* is to be relied upon, Boaden had nine children; this would go some way towards explaining the continual strain on the finances of a jobbing writer.

[174] National Art Library, F.48.E.4, 85.

[175] National Art Library, F.48.E.4, 86.

[176] National Art Library, F.48.E.4, 92.

amount of money out of the publisher over the years. Genuine friendship seems the most likely explanation for Colburn's excessive generosity, but this is precisely what would make further research into the alliance so valuable. Lifting Boaden from obscurity has the potential to add a great deal to our knowledge of Colburn's personal relationships with his authors. It might also help to clarify the extent of Colburn's practice of loaning money to writers who were also friends—a practice that obviously extended beyond his silver-fork celebrity, Benjamin Disraeli.

Despite his affinity for the author of *Vivian Gray*, however, Colburn's ideal author might well have been Thomas Henry Lister. Young, handsome, aristocratic, fashionable, bright, talented, punctilious yet amiable—whatever flaws he had were successfully concealed. He wrote only three novels for Colburn before dying at a comparatively young age, but all were models of the silver-fork school. Adburgham and Sadleir, among others, recognize that he was among the very best silver-fork writers and it is obvious to the reader that he had a better grasp of plot, pace, and narrative structure than many of his more illustrious colleagues.

Thomas Henry Lister (he always used his middle name, to distinguish himself from his father) was born in 1800 to the Listers of Armitage Park, Lichfield, who were relatives of Lord Ribblesdale. His years at Westminster School and Cambridge University made him one of the best-educated Colburn authors as well as one of his most eloquent (and legible) correspondents. With his impressive background and reputation for running with 'a very fast set', Lister was a natural silver-fork author.[177] How exactly he came to write *Granby* and submit it to Colburn in 1826 has yet to be established, but there is the possibility of a pre-existing attachment to the publisher. On the death of his father in 1828, Lister wrote to Colburn about putting an obituary in the *New Monthly*, remarking 'You knew my father, &

---

[177] Adburgham 94.

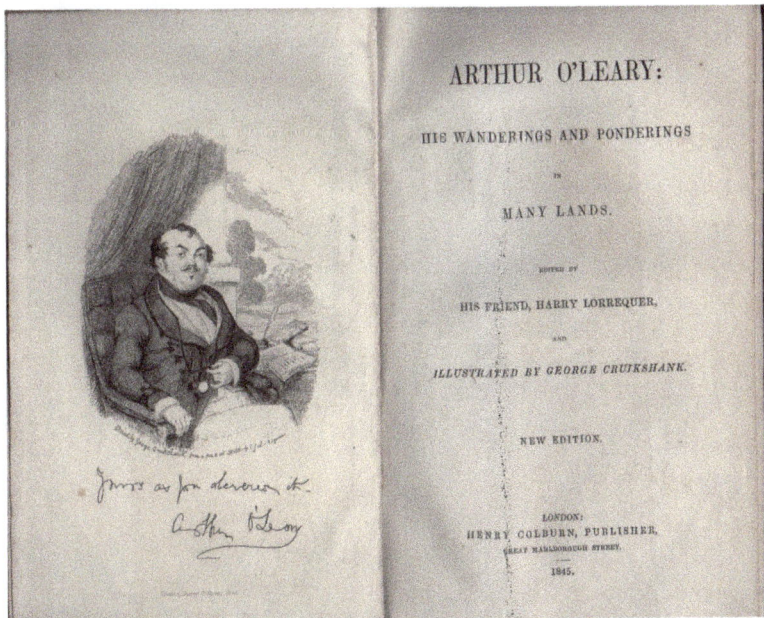

Above: Charles Lever, Arthur O'Leary. *Below:* Benjamin Disraeli, Coningsby.

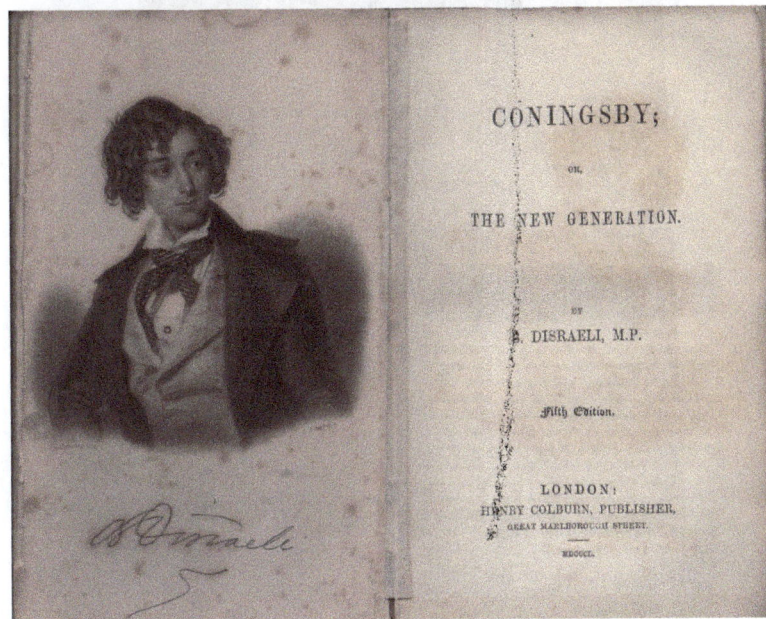

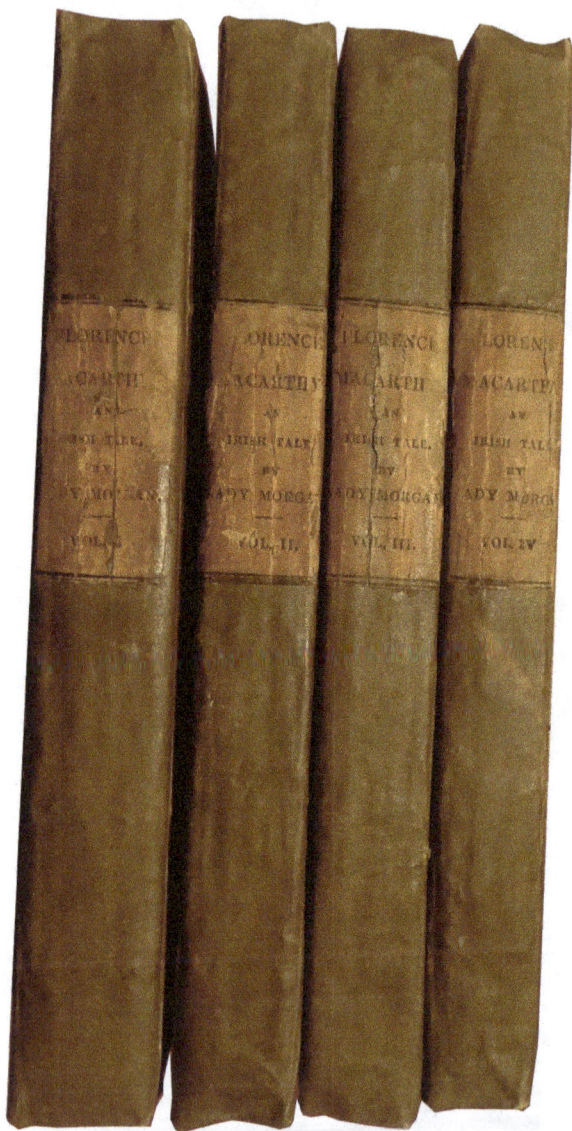

Lady Morgan, Florence Macarthy.

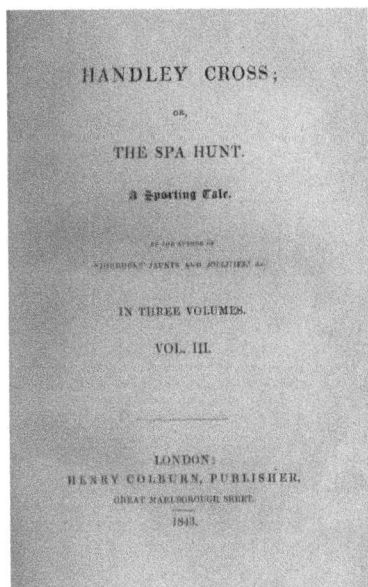

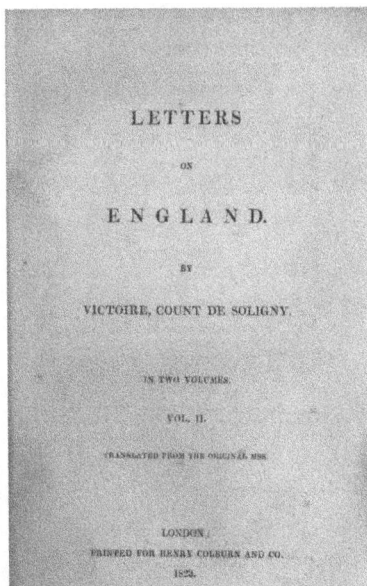

Above left: R.S. Surtees, Handley Cross. *Above right:* Victoire, Count de Soligny, Letters on England. *Below left:* Mrs. C. Gore, Women As They Are. *Below right:* M. de Bourienne, The Life of Napoleon.

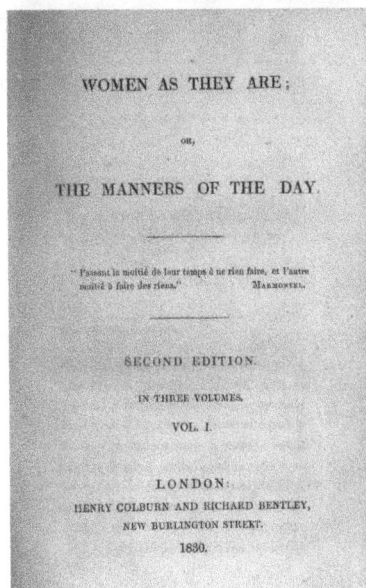

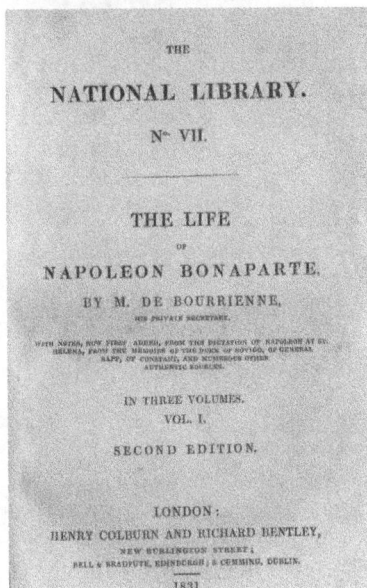

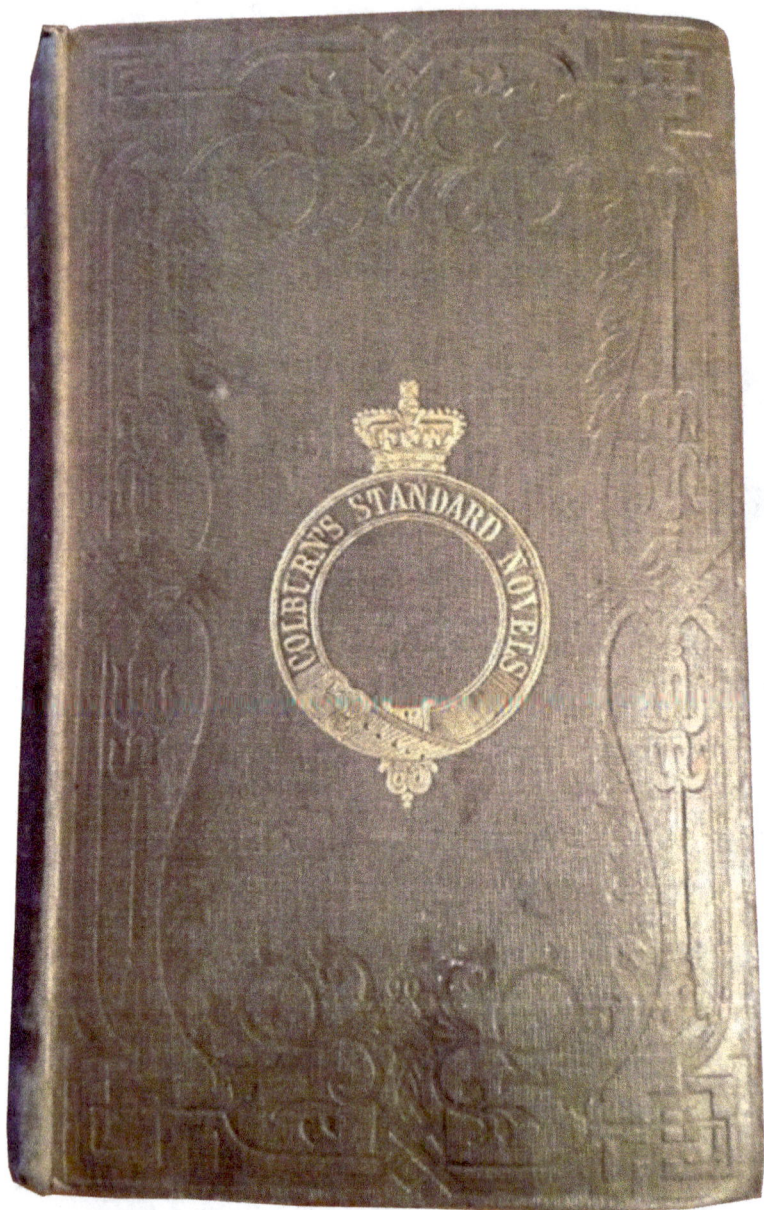

Colburn's Standard Novels.

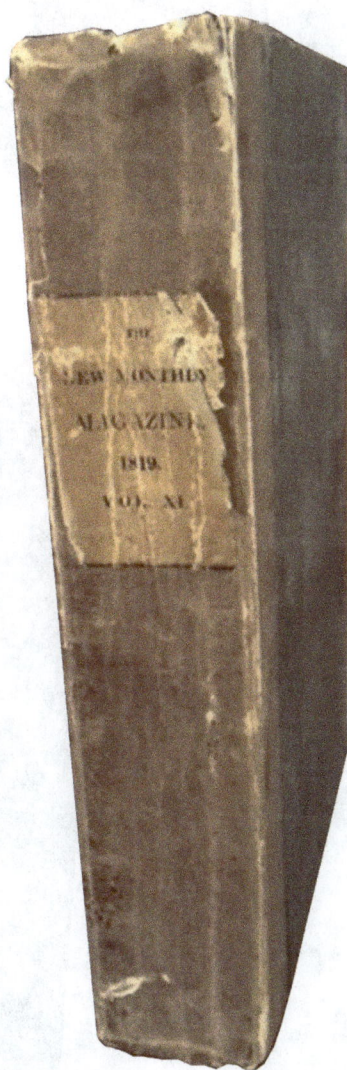

The New Monthly Magazine.

Above: Colburn's Modern and Standard Novels. *Below left:* G.E. Jewsbury, Marian Walters. *Below right:* B. Disraeli, Lord George Bentinck, a Political Biography.

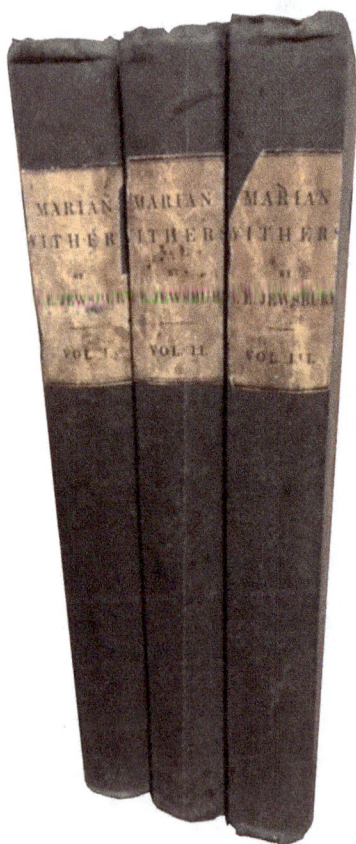

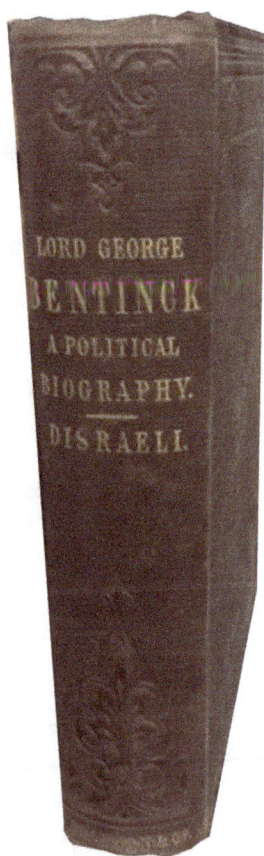

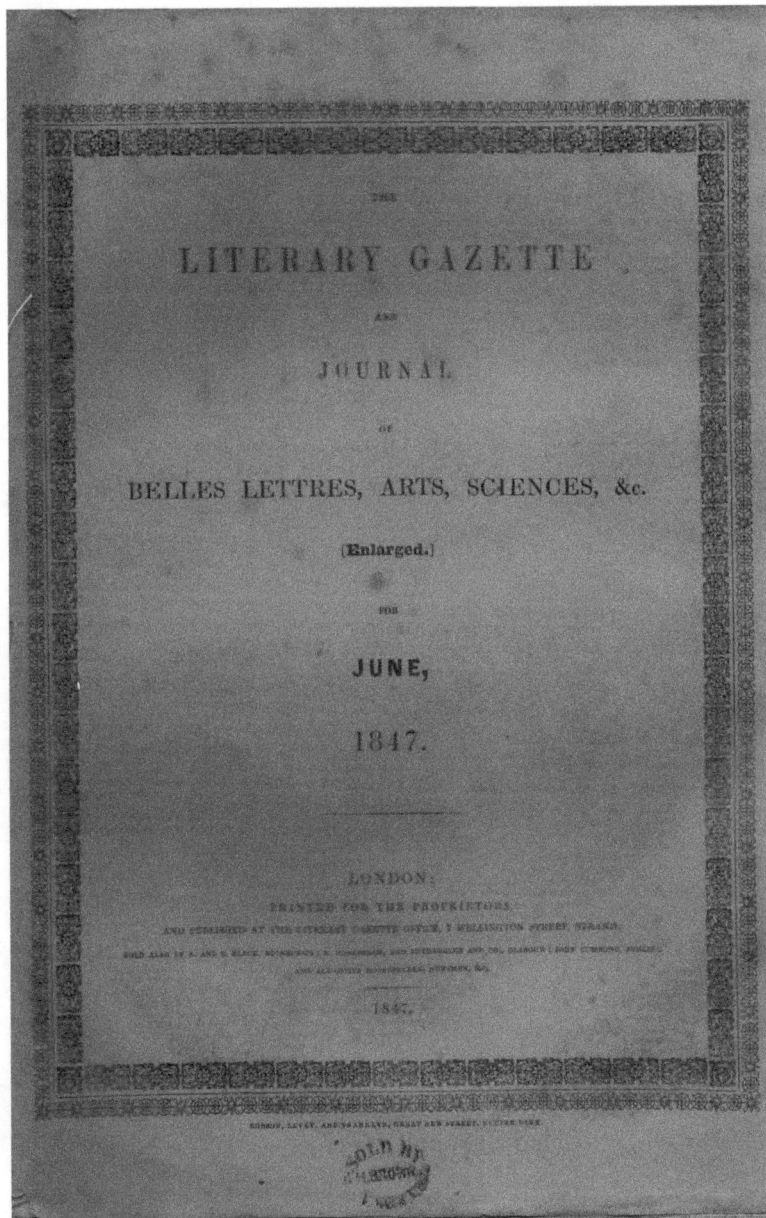

The Literary Gazette.

The Literary Gazette.

H

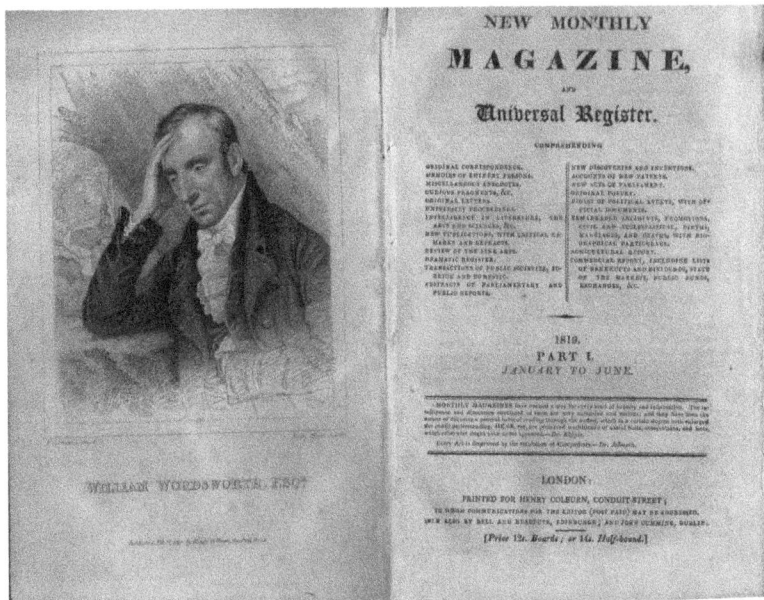

Above: New Monthly Magazine. *Below left:* B. Disraeli, Lord George Bentinck, a Political Biography. *Below right:* Mrs. C. Gore, Men of Capital.

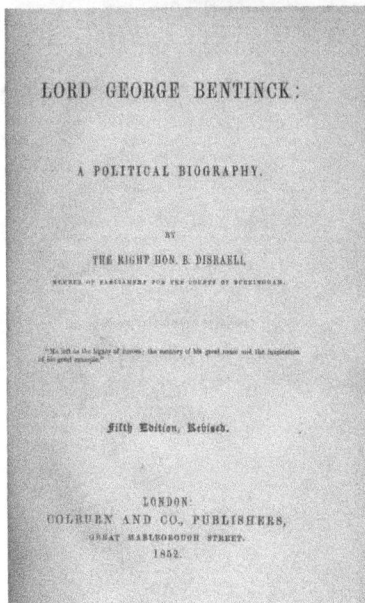

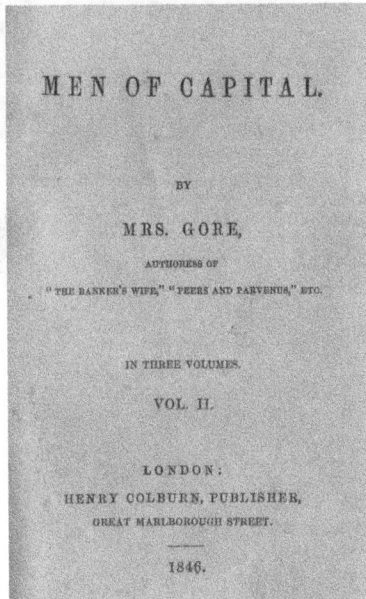

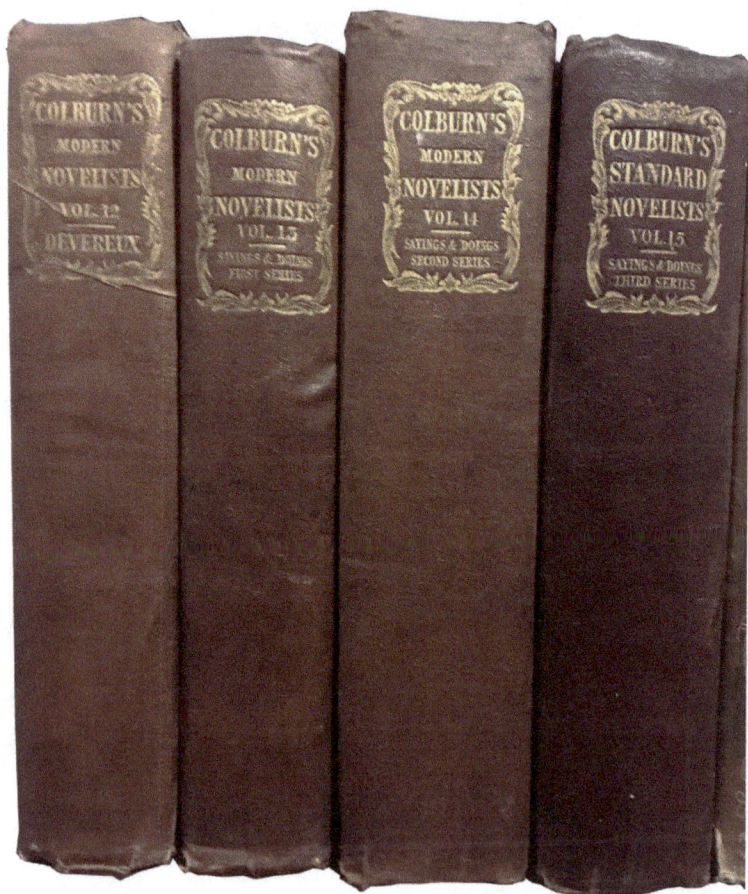

Colburn's Modern Novelists and Standard Novelists.

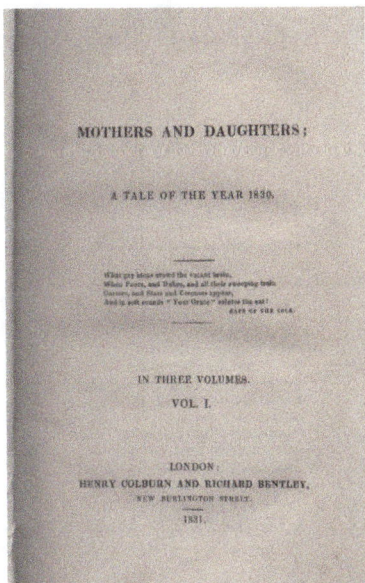

MOTHERS AND DAUGHTERS;

A TALE OF THE YEAR 1830.

IN THREE VOLUMES.
VOL. I.

LONDON:
HENRY COLBURN AND RICHARD BENTLEY,
NEW BURLINGTON STREET.
1831.

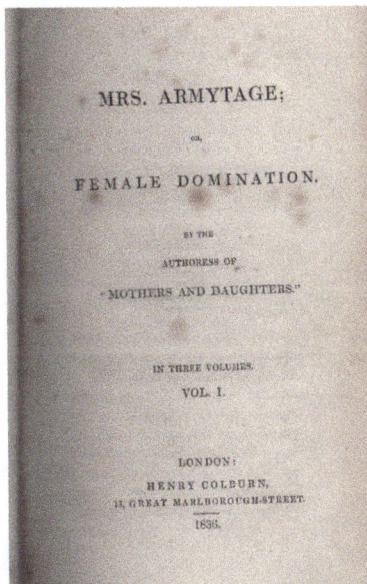

MRS. ARMYTAGE;

OR,

FEMALE DOMINATION.

BY THE

AUTHORESS OF

"MOTHERS AND DAUGHTERS."

IN THREE VOLUMES.
VOL. I.

LONDON:
HENRY COLBURN,
13, GREAT MARLBOROUGH-STREET.
1836.

Above left: Mrs. C. Gore, Mothers and Daughters. *Above right:* Mrs. C. Gore, Mrs. Armytage; or, Female Domination. *Below left:* Bulwer-Lytton, Pelham. *Below right:* Mrs. C. Gore, Pin Money.

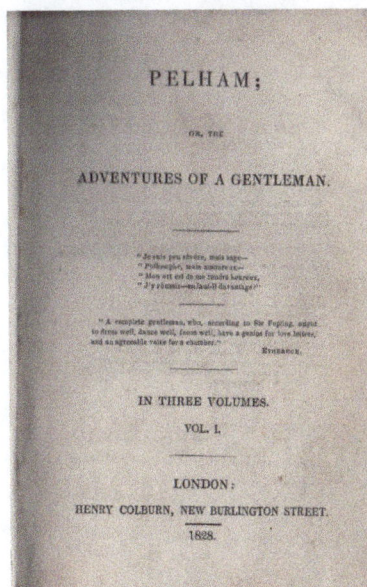

PELHAM;

OR, THE

ADVENTURES OF A GENTLEMAN.

IN THREE VOLUMES.
VOL. I.

LONDON:
HENRY COLBURN, NEW BURLINGTON STREET.
1828.

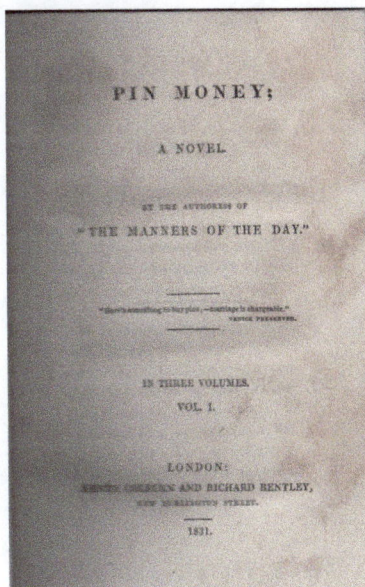

PIN MONEY;

A NOVEL

BY THE AUTHORESS OF

"THE MANNERS OF THE DAY."

IN THREE VOLUMES.
VOL. I.

LONDON:
HENRY COLBURN AND RICHARD BENTLEY,
NEW BURLINGTON STREET.
1831.

K

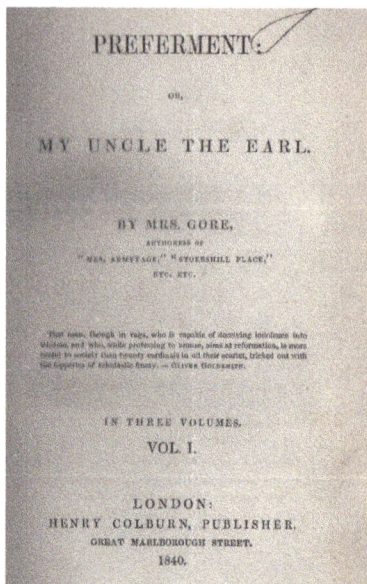

PREFERMENT:

OR,

MY UNCLE THE EARL.

BY MRS. GORE,

AUTHORESS OF
"MRS. ARMYTAGE," "STOKESHILL PLACE,"
ETC. ETC.

IN THREE VOLUMES.
VOL. I.

LONDON:
HENRY COLBURN, PUBLISHER,
GREAT MARLBOROUGH STREET.
1840.

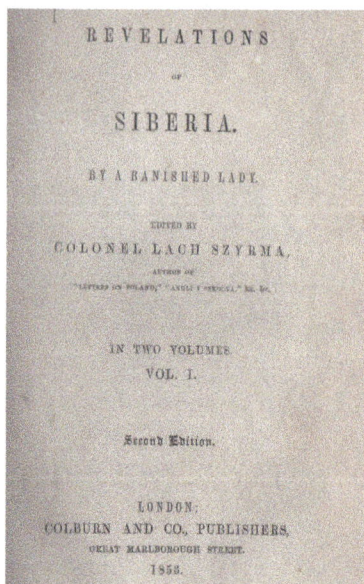

REVELATIONS

OF

SIBERIA.

BY A BANISHED LADY.

EDITED BY
COLONEL LACH SZYRMA,

AUTHOR OF
"LETTERS ON POLAND," "ANGLI POLONICA" &c. &c.

IN TWO VOLUMES.
VOL. I.

Second Edition.

LONDON:
COLBURN AND CO., PUBLISHERS,
GREAT MARLBOROUGH STREET.
1853.

Above left: Mrs. C. Gore, Preferment. *Above right:* Colonel Lach Szyrma (ed.), Revelations of Siberia. *Below left:* Colburn's Modern Novelists. *Below right:* Baroness de Stael-Holstein, Memoirs of the Private Life of My Father.

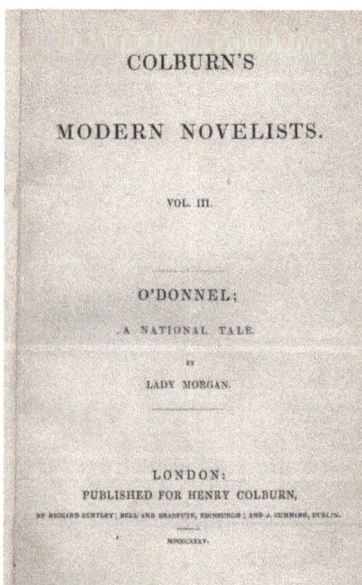

COLBURN'S

MODERN NOVELISTS.

VOL. III.

O'DONNEL;

A NATIONAL TALE.

BY

LADY MORGAN.

LONDON:
PUBLISHED FOR HENRY COLBURN,
BY RICHARD BENTLEY; BELL AND BRADFUTE, EDINBURGH; AND J. CUMMING, DUBLIN.

MDCCCXXXV.

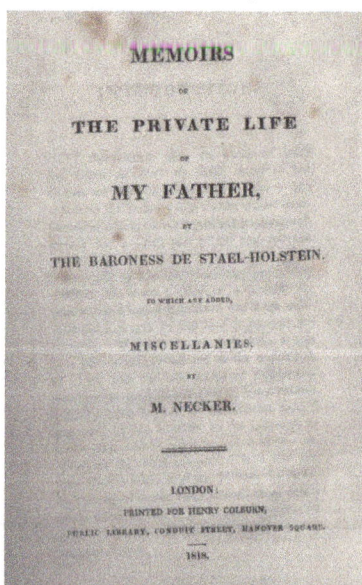

MEMOIRS

OF

THE PRIVATE LIFE

OF

MY FATHER,

BY

THE BARONESS DE STAEL-HOLSTEIN.

TO WHICH ARE ADDED,

MISCELLANIES,

BY

M. NECKER.

LONDON:
PRINTED FOR HENRY COLBURN,
PUBLIC LIBRARY, CONDUIT STREET, HANOVER SQUARE.

1818.

L

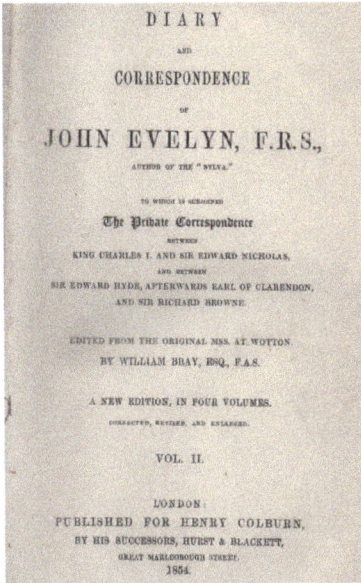

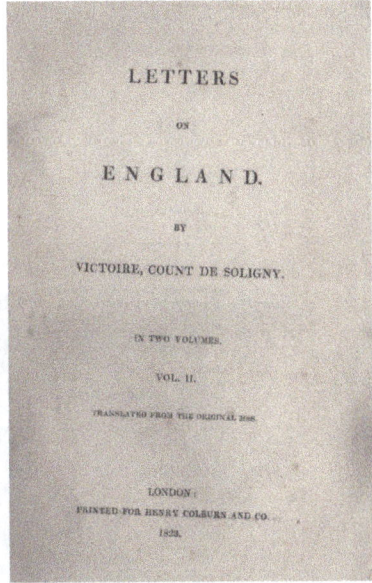

Above left: William Bray (ed.), Diary and Correspondence of John Evelyn, FRS. *Above right:* Victoire, Count de Soligny, Letters on England. *Below:* Bentley's and Colburn's Standard Novels.

M

Lady Morgan (portrait).

Original autograph letter dated July 19 1842 from 13 Great Marlborough
St to J B Burke signed by H. Colburn. Original autograph letter dated
'Monday' from London to Mrs Samuel Carter Hall signed by H Colburn.

Original autograph letter dated July 19 1842 from 13 Great Marlborough St to J B Burke signed by H. Colburn, and Original autograph letter dated 'Monday' from London to Mrs Samuel Carter Hall signed by H Colburn.

I therefore feel assured of your regret'.[178] The question is whether Colburn knew Thomas Lister before 1826 or through publishing his son's works.

Lister's earliest letters to Colburn document a great deal of cordiality between the two men. He makes mention of his publisher's 'very handsome & liberal manner'[179] and touchingly notes that 'the attacks upon yourself I was glad to see have been rebutted'—referring, of course, to the usual criticisms of Colburn's publicity techniques. When offered only £150 for the copyright to his next novel, *Herbert Lacy*, Lister accepted it though he wanted more: 'I feel that I am dealing with a person of character & honour, & have a reliance on your just & fair view of the circumstances'.[180] This was wise, as Colburn soon came round to the view that £300 was more just and fair.[181] The letters also contain a number of typical author-publisher disagreements on titles, corrections, and so forth, but Lister's affability never flags and he usually defers to Colburn's judgment in the end.

After *Granby*, Thomas Henry Lister wrote two novels that did reasonably well without creating the kind of sensation that attended his first work, which had sold out three editions in its first year. *Herbert Lacy* was published in 1828 and *Arlington* in 1832. In the autumn of 1829, Lister sent his only known attempt at drama, *Epicharis,* to Colburn and new partner Richard Bentley. Colburn was on one of his seaside excursions at the time and directed Bentley to stall Lister until the play had been assessed by Ollier, while making clear that he wanted to reach a deal on the piece, 'tho' under any circumstances except keeping a good author to ourselves it cannot be an affair of any moment'.[182] Colburn steeled himself for the play's

---

[178] National Art Library, F.48.E.4, 109.

[179] National Art Library, F.48.E.4, 99–100.

[180] National Art Library, F.48.E.4, 102.

[181] National Art Library, F.48.E.4, 112.

[182] Sadleir Papers, 348, 19.

reception—'if it should be condemned as is very likely and only run three nights'—but still advised Bentley to do a half-profits deal with Lister.[183] *Ephicharis* actually received a favourable reception on stage and went to two print editions the same year.

Throughout this period, Lister's letters raise the questions of how much he knew about Colburn's publicity methods and whether he was troubled by them. Lister was truly displeased with the loss of his anonymity over *Granby*, which he all but blamed on Colburn,[184] but was rather more ambivalent about puffery. He initially seems not to have understood the connection between Colburn's books and periodicals, thanking his publisher for sending him a copy of the 'flattering' review from the *Literary Gazette* and charmingly expressing his hopes that it will help *Granby's* sales.[185] By the time *Herbert Lacy* was ready for publication, however, he may have understood a great deal more than he was willing to admit outright. One can only imagine what Colburn made of the following, written by Lister on 3 December 1827:

> Will you excuse my suggesting a doubt whether much notice in newspaper paragraphs is likely to be beneficial to my forthcoming work. It is a mode of exciting attention which has been so much adopted (as you have doubtless observed) by publishers in your neighbourhood in the case of very inferior books that I think it has begun to produce distrust much more than curiosity.[186]

Was Lister genuinely trying to advise his publisher or was he obliquely criticizing Colburn's infamous publicity schemes? He might have been doing both. Lister's other

---

[183] Sadleir Papers, 348, 18.

[184] National Art Library, F.48.E.4, 110.

[185] National Art Library, F.48.E.4, 104.

[186] National Art Library, F.48.E.4, 111.

letters declare his abiding faith in Colburn's judgment, and the very fact that he never took his fiction to another publisher indicates that he had no real qualms with Colburn's *modus operandi*. Yet he was obviously aware of the 'attacks' on his publisher's methods from other quarters of the trade and may have consequently felt that puffery promised to do more harm than good. Still, the artfulness of these lines is as good a testament to Lister's writing ability as any of his novels.

Interestingly, though not very surprisingly, the *Dictionary of National Biography* erroneously credits Lister with four more novels than he actually wrote, including *Flirtation*, which came from the active pen of Lady Charlotte Bury. It correctly names Lister as the author of *The Life and Administration of Edward, First Earl of Clarendon*, issued in 1837 by Longmans. As this title indicates, Lister's interests turned toward politics as he matured and settled into domestic life with Maria Theresa Villiers, whom he married in 1830. Eventually he served as a commissioner on various inquiries and was named the first registrar-general of England and Wales in 1836. Sadly, he passed away on 5 June 1842, from a cause that has been impossible to discover. Lister was buried in what would eventually be Colburn's final resting place, Kensal Green Cemetery, where he was laid in the catacomb beneath the North Terrace Colonnade.

For all the little details that Colburn's correspondence with Lady Caroline, Boaden and Lister reveals to us, it is perhaps the big picture that matters most. Each writer felt able to communicate directly with the publisher, to speak honestly, and to expect a generous response. Scandal-ridden, penurious, or of the bluest blood, each writer was treated respectfully and chose to maintain the relationship over the course of several years. Was Colburn's relationship with every author so perfect? Evidently not—but neither was Benjamin Disraeli the only one of Colburn's authors who liked and trusted his publisher.

JEWELS AMONG THE SILVER FORKS

The defence of Colburn from the 'slanders' (as they often were) leveled against him invariably cites, as proof-positive of the man's inherent taste and good literary judgement, the two jewels in his crown. Namely the diaries of Samuel Pepys and of John Evelyn, classic works which he introduced to the British reading public in the mid-1820s and whose copyrights he retained even after his retirement from active publishing, so much—it is presumed—did he value them and appreciate their cultural worth. Some background to his acquisition and cultivation of these works, however, dulls the lustre. There is a faint aroma of moral shabbiness tainting Colburn's editions.

On the face of it, one might be surprised at Henry Colburn's discovering, and bringing to light, in their original script, these two privately written seventeenth-century manuscript treasures from the cabinets in which they were stored and forgotten for centuries. And, most significantly, how did he come to 'own' them? There is no evidence that Henry Colburn was an antiquarian or a historian. Or that he was the kind of scholar who could wrestle with Pepys's shorthand. He published both these works while pulsing out a torrent of silver-forkery.

The connection which brought these classics his way was his friendship with William Upcott (1779–1845). Upcott was, indeed, a distinguished antiquarian. He was also one of Colburn's closest friends. It was Upcott, for example, whom he trusted to handle, as intermediary, the tricky business in 1835 of Colburn's return to active London publishing, after the break up from Bentley.

How it happened that Upcott and Colburn became friends can be plausibly deduced from the few biographical details which have survived of the men's youth.

William Upcott was born the only child of a bohemian artist and man of letters, Ozias Humphry. There is, as with Colburn, impenetrable mystery surrounding his birth. He never used his father's surname. 'Upcott' was a middle name. His father (widowed while William was a child) took little interest in his son beyond an allowance to his carers. His mother, Delly Wickers, who may or may not have been legally married to Humphry, died when William was seven. His schooling, in Oxford, was erratic and scanty: but sufficient to have interested him in books, scholarship and museum objects. He may have worked in one of the university city's bookshops or libraries. One suspects he somehow ingratiated himself with university people.

Aged seventeen in 1797, William left for London where his father had helped buy him an apprentice position with the Piccadilly bookseller John Wright. Wright's had been, for generations, a firm specializing in the acquisition, publication and sale of old and rare literary materials—famously those associated with Shakespeare. William was by now too far gone in his teens for a true apprenticeship, and he may simply have been indentured to Wright to learn the ropes of the metropolitan book-world and its rarer items.

In 1800, he moved to the shop of Robert Harding Evans in Pall Mall, where he remained until 1806. Evans was another publisher specializing in rare books and manuscripts. Colburn, of course, was himself apprenticed, and a junior bookseller, in Earle's and Morgan's libraries. Insofar as we know Colburn's age, Upcott was a year or two the older. But working within a few hundred yards of each other, their paths regularly crossing in book delivery duties and at auctions, the youngsters evidently came to know and like each other, forming what would be a lifelong and mutually beneficial friendship.

Upcott was far too talented to remain behind a counter. He left bookselling in 1806, when he took up a position as sub-librarian at the new London Institution. It had been established, by well-meaning Whigs, to offer higher educational, scholarly, and research chances to those disqualified from Oxford and Cambridge (by religious noncomformity, principally; or lack of money, as in Upcott's case). It was a forerunner of London University, twenty years later, and aimed to promote Literature, Philosophy, and the Arts. A founder member of the Institution was the scientist William Haseldine Pepys, a descendant of the diarist. The college Library, which Upcott was instrumental in building, eventually came to contain 70,000 rare volumes.

A DIGRESSION

One may digress briefly, having mentioned London University, to note Colburn's remote, but interesting, connection. The foundation of the University is conventionally dated to 1825 (that extraordinary year). And its moving spirit was a man in Colburn's employment. One can cite the official house history of UCL (as the kernel London University institution came to be called):

Thomas Campbell (1777–1844) was a well-known London literary figure when he proposed the idea for a London University to Lord Brougham, Isaac Goldsmid and other friends in 1824–1825. He was editor of the *New Monthly Magazine* and still famous for his youthful poem, *The Pleasures of Hope*, published in 1799, which expressed his sympathy with political reform, and in particular the anti-slavery movement, in rather trite rhyming couplets. He was one of many Scots involved in the founding of the University of London (later University College London) and brought to bear his experience of the Scottish university system, notably the custom for students to live at home and the wider curriculum than that operating at the two English universities, as well as the freedom from religious tests which excluded non-Anglicans from graduating at Oxford and Cambridge. Campbell had also visited Bonn in 1820, and was impressed by the university system there, particularly by the religious tolerance and the scholarly standards. In September 1825 he went to Berlin with the specific intention of studying the organisation of the University in preparation for setting up the new institution in London.

Colburn (through the generous stipend he paid Campbell, and the easy-going editorial *ménage* he permitted the editor of the *New Monthly*) made it easier for Campbell to assist in founding what became UCL. A harder taskmaster than Colburn might not have approved of an editor's jaunt to look, for purposes which had no relevance to his paid work, at the universities of Germany—although what evidence there is suggests Campbell would not have been much missed from the helm of the *New Monthly*. He was more the figurehead of the vessel.

UPCOTT AND COLBURN

From his father, who died in 1810, Upcott inherited, as the ODNB tells us, a collection of 'extensive correspondence with artists, writers, and men of affairs'. The inheritance triggered a lifelong collecting 'mania' (the word 'madness' is sometimes used) in William, particularly for manuscript remains and autographs. As regards autographs of literary and artistic eminences, Upcott is regarded as the greatest collector of the century—a century which revered these signatory souvenirs. He named his house, in Islington, 'Autograph Cottage'. He was, the evidence suggests, sometimes unscrupulous, with his scissors and with other people's property, in acquiring his treasures.

The connection with Evelyn's diary and his literary remains, and the dubiousness of Upcott's handling of them, is usefully summarized in his entry in the *ODNB:*

> Early in 1813 Upcott was introduced by the antiquary William Bray to Mary, Lady Evelyn, who engaged him to catalogue the library at Wotton, the Evelyn family home in Surrey. There the two men uncovered in a cabinet John Evelyn's famous 'Kalendarium' or diary; Upcott helped Bray to edit the first edition (1818) and in 1825 himself edited Evelyn's *Miscellaneous Works.* During his time at Wotton he also helped himself to a large number of papers and printed books from the library. After Lady Evelyn's death Upcott sanctioned

the publication of an anecdote in which it was stated that she had assured him he was 'welcome to lay aside any [manuscripts] that might add to his own collection' (T. F. Dibdin, *The Library Companion*, 1824, 553); recent research, however, has established not only that Lady Evelyn had no legal authority to make such a grant, but that in May 1815 she demanded the return of all the material Upcott had taken. He failed to restore the property, and it was not until his posthumous sale [in 1845] that the Evelyn family could recover a portion of the manuscripts.

But, whatever murk there is in the background of its journey to the light of print, Colburn produced a series of editions of Evelyn's diary which put the work into circulation. Midwifery can be messy.

The first 'Evelyn', a brutally shortened text, was produced in two quartos, in 1818 (it was published by John Nichols and the Bentleys, to high specification, Upcott supervising). It was well received and followed by a more popular edition in 1825 and an enlarged, five-volume, edition in 1827. All were edited by Bray and Upcott, and published and reprinted in response to solid public demand by Colburn.

PEPYS

It was the 1818 Bray-Upcott Evelyn diary, and the interest it excited, which led to Colburn's coming by the accompanying Pepys's shorthand diary. By the terms of the author's will, the manuscript had been deposited in Magdalene College Cambridge in 1724. It was thought to be impenetrably illegible. Inspired by the success of Colburn's Evelyn edition a stab was made at the manuscript and a couple of pages were laboriously deciphered. A scholarly clergyman, the Revd John Smith (described as 'an impoverished sizar'—i.e., college servant) was commissioned by Richard Neville (later Lord Braybrooke) to translate and transcribe it. Neville's brother, George, was the master of Magdalene College. The family had a curatorial interest. What was required was less transcription than high-order code-breaking (Pepys's key to his shorthand had not yet been discovered). It took Smith three years, 1819–1822. Braybrooke illicitly took total editorial credit. His editorial efforts are regarded as clumsy, erroneous and censorious ('delicate' material was removed on unstated moral principles). Smith, whose transcription proved sound, was barely mentioned. Nor, one suspects, was he generously paid, although the promise of a living was probably held out to him (one did eventually come).

Neville had never taken the trouble to meet him. In subsequent editions Smith's foundational contribution was studiously ignored. The diary was finally published, in two volumes, by Colburn, in 1825. It was well received and reprinted. The edition was thereafter enlarged, culminating in an authoritative text in 1854.

There was an interesting end-story to Colburn and these two valuable copyrights. In 1850, as Colburn was easing into retirement, John Forster set about re-editing the Evelyn Diary. It took him two years. Its main claim was that he found unpublished material in Upcott's papers and brought a higher level of annotation.

The task evidently brought him into social intercourse with Colburn. And he seems to have been able to bring Dickens, whose great friend he was, to the Colburn dining table. Dickens was, with *David Copperfield* (and later with *Great Expectations*) interested in 'diaristic' narration. His interest in the 17th century otherwise was not large. And his respect for Colburn, insofar as one can detect it, was even less large.

Forster's edition was published in 1854 and 1857, and sold on to various cheap 'libraries'. Forster was interested in more than Colburn's literary remains. When the publisher died, Forster married his widow, who had inherited the two great copyrights. With the ringing of the marriage bells, they passed into the possession of Forster, who looked after them conscientiously.

It is clear that Colburn did not own the pristine copyrights of the Evelyn and Pepys diaries—he owned his serial editions: 'versionings', as bibliographers call them. But since these transcriptions were the only versions of the texts available, he was sole supplier. No other publisher was willing to sponsor new transcribing (not all scribes would be as cheap as John Smith) and the editorial apparatus required. And, one cannot but note, there were two aggrieved persons behind these money spinners: John Smith and Lady Bray, both of whom might legitimately think themselves badly treated. And Colburn? He was, as ever, Henry Colburn.

RICHARD BENTLEY, PUBLISHER

Richard Bentley later recalled that he first met Henry Colburn through the antiquarian William Upcott, who was reading the proofs of Evelyn's *Diary*, which his uncle, John Nichols, was printing for Colburn. It was an important book for the publisher. Around the same time, the Bentley brothers struck out on their own. Documentation survives showing that Colburn was an early patron of their new firm. He evidently approved of the quality of their work: hence the commission in 1821 to print his *New Monthly Magazine*. They were entrusted with his *editions de luxe*, illustrated books, top-listed fiction, and when it was launched in 1829, the *Court Journal*.

The two parties were, even at this stage, closer than publishers and printers usually were. In October 1822, Colburn took Richard with him on a business trip to Paris. It indicates closeness—a closeness which, Sadleir suggests, rather worried Samuel Bentley. On moral grounds, presumably. Sadleir cites a letter from Samuel to Richard, while his younger brother was in Paris, encouraging him to learn about French printing techniques. The letter closes: 'I don't say any more about your stay—you know my sentiments on that head. I suppose you and Mr C. will return together'. It could be read as a neutral comment, or a sour disapproval of 'Mr C' and the possible temptations for a young man in the French capital.[187]

---

[187] Sadleir Papers, 360, 5b.

There is no surviving material recording the personal relationship between Colburn and the Bentley brothers during the fraught 1820s. The question which arises is why Colburn should, on his part, have wanted partnership. He was, by nature, a lone wolf. The British book trade by this historical point had formed into its modern three separate parts: book selling, book printing and binding, and book publishing. Publishers commissioned printers: there was no commercial advantage in getting into bed with them.

It has been suggested that Colburn was in debt (not implausible, given the extent of his spending on puffery) and needed the influx of cash that a new partner would bring. The obvious flaw in that argument, however, is that the indenture signed at the very beginning of the partnership provided for Colburn's retirement at the end of that partnership in three years' time; Colburn was quirky, but not crazy enough to stop working just as he was paying off his debts. The other flaw in the argument is that Richard Bentley, not otherwise known for his discretion about Colburn's personal affairs, never mentioned or even intimated that Colburn was in debt in 1829. What Bentley *did* later admit was that, in a financial crisis that hit the firm in 1831, Colburn bailed them out by providing more than his fair share of capital.[188] The partnership was not a money-making scheme for the senior partner.

The simplest explanation for why he initiated the partnership is that he was unwell and wanted to get away from his exhausting business concerns. At the time of the partnership agreement with Bentley, Colburn was forty-five and had been in business for more than half his life. His letters at this time demonstrate that he was troubled by ear and tooth ailments that prevented him from sleeping.[189] London's air, especially in high summer, caused chronic discomfort. He was more comfortable at the coast, a long

---

[188] British Library, Add.MS.46632A, 38–43.
[189] Sadleir Papers, 351, 7.

coach ride away (since this was before the convenience of rail travel). How serious a worry health was to Colburn is uncertain, but the indenture agreement he signed with Bentley made it clear that he would let the younger man do the donkey work, in preparation for handing the business over to Bentley in 1832.

Why the origins and purpose of the partnership should ever have been a mystery is itself the real puzzle. The 1829 indenture signed by Colburn and Bentley that has been sitting among the Bentley Papers for decades is entirely predicated on Colburn going into semi-retirement at the end of three years together. It defined what his semi-retirement would entail (namely, managing his journals and pre-partnership copyrights) and restricted him from becoming a direct competitor to his successor.[190] When the partnership did, in fact, reach its conclusion in 1832, Colburn restated the plan he had made with Bentley to James Fennimore Cooper: 'I hasten to state to you [...] that I went into the partnership with him for three years with the express intention of so retiring at the end of the term'.[191]

In his unpublished obituary of Colburn, Richard Bentley is unambiguous about how he came to be the successor to Colburn's business. He was, of course, writing without fear of contradiction by his former partner, later his enemy, in a spirit of *nil nisi bonum:*

> In 1828–9 I learnt accidentally that Colburn was about to dispose of his business. He had spoken to Alderman Key, to the Magnays, and others. As our business with him was very important—about £3,000 to £3,500 a year—I did not like the idea of its going into hands adverse to us. Therefore I spoke to him about it. He

---

[190] The indenture document is discussed briefly below and at greater length in Appendix Three.

[191] British Library, Add.MS.46632A, 55.

was much pleased. I offered it to brother Samuel, who declined; then to brother Will, who also declined it. Then I said I would take it myself.

The indenture that Bentley signed with Henry Colburn on 3 June 1829 was to go into effect on 31 August of that year.[192] It is as dull as legal documents invariably are and a detailed outline and analysis is given as Appendix Three. What may be noted here is that the terms of partnership were, on the face of it, inequitable. Bentley bought in for £2,500. He almost certainly did this by selling his share of the family printing firm: to his brother Samuel, presumably. Colburn was to scoop off three-fifths of the publishing profit, while Bentley undertook 'all the active part of the said business, and all the labour and trouble of carrying on and conducting the same'. Colburn's position was that of managing director, superintending the activity of his junior partner. It would very much be *Colburn* and Bentley.

By the terms of the indenture Bentley was allowed to reside in the part of the house on New Burlington Street not taken up by the business and was to have the lease (and expense) transferred to his name after the dissolution of the partnership. Until then he was, effectively, Colburn's tenant. His living 'over the shop' meant long hours.

---

[192] British Library, Add.MS.46632A, 3–13.

'ONE OF THE BEST BUSINESSES IN LONDON'

It was always intended that Bentley would take over the running of the day-to-day affairs, freeing Colburn to rest at home or by the sea as his medical conditions required. Unfortunately, his health worsened to the point that he required such rest precisely at the time of Bentley's induction into the partnership. Colburn thought that this was no coincidence and wrote to Bentley that the stress of the upheaval was exacerbating his medical complaints, noting: 'I am so very unwell with the great exertions I have been making these several days past'.[193] In the early months of the partnership, he was often forced to rest and recuperate at his new home in Northumberland Place or near the sea in Hastings or Margate.

When Colburn was at work both immediately before and after his new partner's arrival, he continued his publishing speculations and began preparing the house on New Burlington Street for its new resident. What Bentley was doing during August 1829 is unknown, but he most certainly was not liaising with Colburn. The publisher summed up the situation in a letter dated 31 August: 'I have much to say relative to the *conduct of the business* and *regret much* it has been impossible for me to find leisure

---

[193] Sadleir Papers, 351, 8.

when you have been in town to enter upon it'.[194] Once the partnership began in earnest and Colburn found himself too unwell to conduct business in person, he attempted to rectify matters by writing letter after letter to Bentley explaining the many details of the operation. He could not, however, outline all of Bentley's tasks without seeming to badger and mistrust the new partner. Colburn at least tried his best to sound encouraging and appreciative of Bentley's efforts, writing from Hastings at the end of September that

> I have at last really made my escape & left all my troubles upon your shoulders pro tempore & from what I have already seen I must confess you seem to be able to bear them better & lessen them sooner than I could do, tho you may always rely on all my assistance whether in town or country.[195]

Still, leaving the novice publisher unaided and perhaps just a little overwhelmed was a most unpropitious way to begin the partnership. Face-to-face communication was required, but it rarely happened.

It was at this early stage that Bentley began to oversee the refurbishment of 8 New Burlington Street. Disputes about the refurbishment—by letter—forecast, comically, the pettiness which would blight the partnership: the inability to agree about anything, however minor. First, they argued about the skylights in the counting house (necessary for the clerks), with Bentley preferring them small and round while Colburn wanted them large and square, since 'we may as well get a good light for the dark winter days'.[196] Frugal to the core, he worried about the expense of candles. There was an argument about stucco,

---

194 Sadleir Papers, 348, 14.
195 Sadleir Papers, 348, 19.
196 Sadleir Papers, 348, 10.

which Colburn recommended and Bentley had executed at great expense—though not enough to prevent Colburn from that he had 'never witnessed such a shameful job'.[197] Bentley bitterly complained, in a marginal note on Colburn's letter, that it was he (Colburn) who had commissioned the plasterer. When the renovations were at last finished, the bills paid, and the minutiae settled, Colburn and Bentley got started on more important matters. They began to argue about publishing.

---

[197] Sadleir Papers, 348, 15.

LOVE AND BUSINESS: A DIGRESSION

One knows tantalizingly little about Colburn's personal life—but one possible explanation for his eye being off his business at this period is less health matters than affairs of the heart. In this interval of mysterious separation from London, Bentley, and business, Colburn was forging another partnership: scarcely longer lasting than that with Bentley and just as fraught. Marriage, in a word.

Contemporary commentators refrain from naming his bride. Colburn himself simply calls her 'Mrs C.' on the two occasions he mentions her in surviving letters to Bentley. Her name is, however, on the marriage licence allegation that Colburn filed at the Vicar-General's Office on 30 September 1830. It stated Henry Colburn's intention to wed Mary Daysh Campbell (any relation to Thomas? probably not) of the parish of St. Pancras. Otherwise the document is uninformative. The couple married shortly afterwards in Marylebone.

Colburn's editorial assistant S. C. Hall offers a few intriguing sentences about this woman of mystery in his 1883 memoir. He recalls spending an evening a week at the Colburn home discussing plans for the upcoming number of the *New Monthly Magazine*:

> [Colburn] was then, though somewhat aged, newly married, and to a wife who made him miserable. She had originally kept a small circulating library. Colburn

married her, and by her habits she rendered both him and his home wretched. I once saw her fling a teapot at his head, and she died at last a victim to intemperance.[198]

Cyrus Redding, the *New Monthly's* long-serving sub-editor, completes the minimum of what we know about Mary Colburn née Campbell with a fleeting reference to her in *Yesterday and Today.* He offers the tantalizing information: 'we had heard of Colburn's marriage, but the lady was invisible'.[199] Redding is uncertain as to what became of Colburn's wife, saying only that she was thought to have died in Paris, not long after the marriage. Why Paris?

With reference to the 'small' circulating library she appears to have kept, most likely near Oxford Street (which would explain how Colburn met her) he offers the following epigram by Lady Morgan's husband, Sir Thomas:

> When Colburn wedded the tenth muse,
> Who lends out novels, plays, reviews,
> He could not, for his little life,
> Select more cunningly his wife.
> He rightly judged his situation,
> His own books wanting circulation
> And placed a dame at his devotion
> Whose books are in perpetual motion.[200]

The union, Morgan suggests in this lame lampoon, was a business affair, not a love match. Colburn had money problems at this period and perhaps both partnerships were financially motivated. But if he were obliged to marry the proprietress of a small circulating library, his financial

---

[198] Hall, op cit., I, 316.

[199] Redding, op cit., III, 72.

[200] Redding, op cit., III, 74.

difficulties must have been severe indeed.

Bentley's obituary of Colburn adds a few other, juicier, details. Colburn, he says 'kept a woman for some years who kept a library called Campbell's Library in Rathbone Place' north of Oxford Street. She was his mistress (a 'kept' woman). In autumn 1830, Bentley recalls, his partner appeared at the New Burlington Street office with 'a singular expression of countenance'. It prompted Bentley to enquire what was wrong. After an uneasy pause, Colburn announced his intention to be married and asked Bentley to give the bride away. Accordingly, Colburn sent a coach round for his junior partner on the appointed day, and Bentley escorted Miss Mary Campbell to Marylebone Church where he signed the marriage register.

This account, with its witness to the groom's unease and the absence of the bride's friends or family, would be even more mystifying than those of Hall and Redding had not Bentley followed it up with few more personal comments. The obituary account continues, 'The marriage was unfortunate. I suppose it is the fate of such marriages that it should be so. At any rate, Colburn did what I think was the part of a Christian and worthy member of society.'

The presumable reason behind this 'unfortunate' union is clear enough: Mary Campbell was pregnant. This would explain the 'invisibility'. Bentley finishes his account:

> This Mrs. Colburn took to drinking, and in her fits was very violent, and was a fruitful cause of trouble to the poor man. Finally she went to Boulogne, where she resided in apartments, and where, having abundance of cognac, she soon cut her way to death. He allowed her £300 a year there.

Like the other partnership, it ended unhappily.

THE PARTNERSHIP

Despite their tiffs, rifts, rows and differences of opinion, Bentley quickly adapted to Colburn style and practice as a publisher. *Fraser's*—malevolent as ever—called them the 'Princes of Puffing': one as bad as the other.[201] As always, the most expensive item in the outgoing expenses of the firm was advertisement. Edward Morgan estimated an expenditure of £27,000 during their three years together.[202] This, by the standards of the day, was indeed 'princely'. Dangerously so.

Among the Sadleir papers are precise instructions to Bentley as to how puffing should be done—who should receive gratis copies (and how many), who flattered, who (editors in Colburn-connected journals) coerced. Who, bluntly, bribed or bullied into good opinions.

Occasionally there were blunders. Colburn and Bentley turned down Carlyle's *Sartor Resartus,* for example, which was a mistake. Colburn probably instigated the rejection on the grounds of the book's vitriolic satire against Lytton's dandyism. Lytton was an author whose clientship he treasured. Another blunder, so to call it, is instructive as to how business was done over the men's three years together.

One of the early novels Colburn and Bentley published

---

[201] Feb 1831, 113.

[202] Sadleir Papers, 350, 2.

was the enticingly titled *The Separation* by Lady Charlotte Bury—one of the more prolific silver-fork authors and a favourite of Colburn's, always an admirer of Lady Whatever. *The Separation* turned out to be a crude rehash of Bury's *Self-Indulgence* (1812), dating from before her long association with Colburn. *The Court Journal* innocently remarked the resemblance (which was painful, given who the magazine's founder was). But it was William Jerdan in the *Literary Gazette* (another Colburn property) who spelled out the deception in detail and, in trying to clear Colburn and Bentley's name, made the grave error of referring to their puffery directly and, as it turned out, damagingly to the new firm's character. Colburn and Bentley was, readers of the *Gazette* were free to conclude, old Colburn wine in new bottles.

Among the Sadleir Papers are a handful of letters from Colburn to Bentley touching on this debacle and making clear that neither man had for a moment suspected what Bury was up to. Colburn took charge of the crisis. He could have written to the journals letters of exculpation but he shrewdly decided to let Bury explain what had gone wrong, privately. She did not respond to the invitation. Colburn duly concluded that 'all the disgrace must fall upon her', but decided to let things lie.[203] It would blow over. Such things always did. 'Do not let us magnify the affair', he sagely instructed Bentley.[204] But he felt a grudge—specifically against Jerdan, whom he had himself appointed all those years ago. It was not the first time, he told Bentley, that the editor of the *Literary Gazette* had shown his 'cloven hoof'.[205]

---

[203] Sadleir Papers, 349, 4a.

[204] Ibid.

[205] Sadleir Papers, 349, 2.

PUFF, PUFF TOGETHER

Richard Bentley's apologists routinely argue that he bought into Colburn's firm without knowing the true extent of his puffery and, once in the joint firm, distanced its character from his partner's worst excesses in that line.

That Bentley was ignorant of Colburn practices is a preposterous allegation: anyone who read any of the literary journals knew all about his puffery, and Bentley, being one of the *New Monthly Magazine's* printers, must have seen plenty of Colburnian puffery at first hand.

Neither does the second apology hold up. Bentley, whatever his private reservations, went along with his partner's trade practices. The letters still extant make clear that Bentley acquiesced to whatever puffing instructions Colburn dispatched. Nor is there any surviving evidence—in the Bentley Papers, in the Sadleir Papers, or elsewhere—of Bentley contradicting Colburn's instructions, remonstrating with him, or otherwise expressing his moral disapproval. Nor does Bentley refer to his being coerced into bad ways in his generally frank obituary of Colburn.

Clinching Bentley's acquiescence are successful puffery campaigns carried out under the joint auspices of 'Colburn and Bentley', which induced *Fraser's* to pluralize Colburn's usual epithet and dub the partners 'the Princes of Puffing'.[206] The princely sums the firm spent on

---

[206] Feb. 1831, 113.

151

advertising (on which Bentley must have signed off) speak for themselves: Edward Morgan estimated an expenditure of £27,000 during their three years together and most other sources agree on an annual figure between £9,000 and £10,000.[207]

That puffery was simply standard practice for the firm is revealed in some detail by a couple of documents among the Sadleir Papers, prepared by Colburn on 19 October 1829 for Bentley and the New Burlington Street staff. Colburn drew up a list of those to whom review copies of Cooper's *Borderers* should be sent, explaining to Bentley,

> I have much neglected these points & am anxious now that they should be attended to in the most regular & systematic way, for they are next in importance to our own early paragraphs, besides that the volunteer notices will furnish me with materials for new paragraphs.[208]

The term 'volunteer notices' is particularly interesting. Colburn obviously uses it to denote legitimate reviews by the magazines' own staff, as differentiated from regular 'notices', which were provided by the publisher himself. But then, according to this letter, even volunteer notices would be turned into regular notices eventually.

The plan or system that Colburn laid out consists of some lists and a few general points.[209] The lists are directed to Mr. Cochrane and name the various journal editors and reviewers to whom 'gratis copies' of various books should be sent. One list is exclusively for Cooper's *The Borderers*, with Colburn pointing out that such a list needs to be constructed for each individual title, with variations dependent on 'the nature of the work'. A second list enumerates those lucky few who should receive copies of *everything*. This group naturally

---

[207] Sadleir Papers, 350, 2.

[208] Sadleir Papers, 351, 2.

[209] Sadleir Papers, 348, 5–6.

consists of representatives of Colburn's own journals: the *New Monthly*, *Court Journal*, *Sunday Times*, *Literary Gazette* and—one surprise—the editor of the *Spectator*, possibly a personal acquaintance.

At this point, Colburn feels the need to intervene with an explanation marked 'Very important':

> In addition to the above, two notices of each Book with review about 1/3 of a Column should be written by Mr Ollier or Mr Roscoe for insertion in the Courier & Globe, whose editors have not time to write reviews. These 2 notices should be accompanied by Copies & a note from Mr Colburn (for the present).
>
> There is never any hurry for those 2 notices as our paragraphs will be operating at first effectually in these and the general newspapers, but it is particularly desirable that copies for perusing should go early to the weekly papers, as marked.

This is a clinching summary of Colburn's puffing tactics in the press outlets he controlled or could bribe. One particularly relishes the note of altruism struck by the publisher providing reviews for editors who 'have not time' to write their own. And Colburn also seems to be gearing up for the eventual handing over of power to Bentley when he says that he will write the accompanying notes 'for the present'. In course of time, Bentley will take over the reins himself.

The final list in Colburn's plan takes the form of a chart, with an extensive catalogue of reviewers and editors on one side, Colburn and Bentley's five latest titles across the top, and a series of ticks denoting who was to receive what. Theodore Hook, editing *John Bull* at this time, received one of each, as did the stern John Gibson Lockhart at the *Quarterly Review*. Still in Colburn's good books was Lady Morgan, who was to receive two of the titles with the 'publisher's compliments'. Perhaps thinking of this author reminded Colburn to say a few words to Cochrane about the author's place in the puffing system, for he adds: 'Authors—q[uer]y, have they any influential friends to whom it would be worthwhile sending copies? In case of 1/2 profits, charge copies to authors'.

The first part of that directive comes as no surprise, but the second part reveals that extensive puffery—particularly the sending out of gratis copies—was not to be undertaken for every book. Colburn puffed extravagantly but not recklessly, always mindful of his own expenses and weighing up the likely return on them.

WHAT THE PARTNERSHIP ACHIEVED

Calamitous as the personal relationship of Colburn and Bentley would eventually become, their union had significance for the long-term evolution of British publishing. Their 1830–31 list continues Colburn's late 1820s momentum, shrugging off the crash (and nervousness about the forthcoming Reform Bill) with 119 titles. The mixture is exactly as in 1829, with sixty works of fiction, forty-five of them three-deckers, most of them 'fashionable' in tone. All of them directly commissioned by Colburn.

Richard Bentley brought no new flavour (only, it could be claimed, better business order) to the firm's established proceedings. The handful of titles with clear lasting value are *Paul Clifford* (1830, see above) and the even more incendiary Newgate Novel, *Eugene Aram* (1831), Disraeli's *Young Duke* (1831), John Galt's *Bogle Corbet* (1831), Frederick Marryat's *Newton Forster* (1831), Theodore Hook's *Maxwell* (1831), Mary Shelley's *Fortunes of Perkin Warbeck* (1830), and Trelawney's *Adventures of a Younger Son* (1831).

Mrs. Gore remained the most reliable of silver-fork performers with *Mothers and Daughters, The Historical Traveller, Pin Money,* and *The Tuileries*—all published in 1831, a typically fertile year for the 'queen' of the genre she had made her own. She was supported by the ever-reliable Lady Charlotte Bury (no longer in disgrace), who produced another tidal stream of high-life romance, with a stronger roman à clef element than Gore's. Over the same period, John Burke established himself as the authoritative chronicler of British nobility, and the partnership launched Thomas Hood's *Comic Annual* (1830). Burke and Hood were to remain loyal (possibly shackled) to Colburn after the partnership's break-up.

THE STANDARD NOVELS: THE PARTNERSHIP'S SOLE MONUMENT

With twenty-five years of trading behind him, Colburn had a mass of copyrights and the partnership embarked on various 'library' schemes to push cheap reprints. Their most successful innovation in this line was the 'Standard Novels'. This series established the two-tier arrangement by which a 'Library' three-decker, at a wholly deterrent (for the average purchaser) cost of 31/6d was followed, after a year or so, by a one-volume reissue at 6s. It was a more manageable (although still stiff) price. In fact, the libraries liked the one-volume form for works whose day had passed, but still had residual appeal. They created shelf-space.

Exactly whose idea the Standard Novel was is disputed. According to Sadleir (for whom Colburn can do no good), it must have been Bentley's. Gettmann suggests John Burke. Charles Knight—himself a pioneer of cheap books—claims that he came to Colburn with the idea in the mid-1820s, which is plausible. Suggestion, one should note, is very different from doing. Probably no single 'inventor' of the Standard Novel innovation can be isolated, but Colburn surely deserves a part credit for the initiative.

The realization that there was money to be made from the standardized reprint was, for a certainty, inspired by Robert Cadell's 'Magnum Opus' reprint series of the works of Walter Scott—one of the means by which the great novelist recovered from the catastrophic financial damage he incurred for himself and his publishers in 1825. Scott's copyrights were acquired at auction by the novelist and Cadell in 1827 (they cost a massive £8,500). The oeuvre was then gathered for the so-called 'Magnum Opus' collective reissue in June 1828. Colburn would have been part of the book-world looking at the Cadell-Scott speculative venture with professional curiosity. A prospectus was issued in February 1829, and there was intensive advertising. By the end of 1829, 35,000 copies a month of the 5s reprints were being sold. Forty-eight volumes were produced in the years 1829–1833. It was, Scott declared, an 'El Dorado'. Colburn was never one to withhold his pitchfork from any handy gold mine. At the very least, Colburn and Bentley took over from Cadell the pulsing monthly issue—it made five or six shillings less painful an outlay.

Moreover, a reprint series of the Standard Novels kind was an ideal way to make use of Colburn's substantial stockpile of old copyrights. From the series' inception to the end of their partnership, they managed to produce nineteen volumes, some of which qualify as classic works. Among them were five novels by James Fenimore Cooper, two by William Godwin, and several titles by the sisters Anne Maria and Jane Porter. All of these had sold reasonably well for Colburn on their initial release (though for some of the Cooper titles, such as *The Last of the Mohicans*, this was their initial British release, thus slightly fudging the reprint label). By the time the partners split, eleven of the first twelve volumes had turned a profit and were still selling, while the later volumes were also heading for the same profitable outcome.[210]

One example will serve to show the commercial value of the Standard Novel line. In 1832, Bentley bought five of Jane Austen's copyrights for the paltry sum of £210,

---

[210] Erickson, op cit., 151.

outright. For forty years these novels ran, remuneratively, in the Standard Novels, a brand-name Bentley retained after the split, at a few shillings (the purchase cost was drastically reduced over the years).

In 1875, Anthony Trollope, in his autobiography, declared that *Pride and Prejudice* was the greatest novel in the English language. It was by then an uncontroversial judgement. The universal availability, and supreme status, of Jane Austen's masterpiece—at affordable price (for small libraries and middle-class customers)—could not have happened without, what else?, Colburn and Bentley's (put it, perhaps, the other way round) Standard Novels.

The series sold solidly for decades after it was inherited by Bentley. The vast bulk of that inexhaustible stream of revenue returned to him. The legacy of the Standard Novels survives, to this day, in the hardback / paperback dualism.

DISSOLUTION

The relationship between Colburn and Bentley had been doomed, in any long-term way, from its inception. The men were temperamentally irreconcilable. As Royal Gettmann observes (from an extensive examination of surviving papers), Colburn was, by nature, less than scrupulous in his business dealings; Bentley was, by nature, punctilious to a fault. A worrier, not a book trade warrior. Colburn, shortly after they joined forces, had, belligerently, dragged the new firm into the mud with a ludicrous feud against his former darling, Lady Morgan, in 1830. Her offence was to write a new book on France with his rivals (as his old friends now were) Saunders and Otley. They were all three of them vipers who had been warmed in the Colburn bosom. He promptly advertised (using the new firm's title) a bargain selection of Morgan's books under the outrageous banner headline: 'Lady Morgan at Half-Price!', and proclaimed, privately, that he had always lost money in dealing with the faithless authoress. Complicated lawsuits ensued, the publicity of which must have mortified Bentley.

The terms of the original Indenture agreement were proving to be grievously unbalanced. External stresses made the union even more frictional. The period preceding the 1832 Reform Bill was deadly for publishing. The book trade, with its long financial return lines, hates socio-political instability. By autumn 1831, the firm was in crisis; bankruptcy was averted only by Colburn's selling his share in the *Sunday Times* and the *Court Journal*. Desperate remedies.

Looking back, Bentley attributed this financial crisis to three factors: a large 'dead' stock of 'printed unpublished books' hanging in the warehouse from Colburn's earlier pre-partnership career; the failure of various non-fiction series and 'libraries' the firm had ventured on; and a remainder sale that earned just over half of what Thomas Tegg, the famous disposer of 'broken books' (who had enriched himself clearing up the debris of 1825), would have paid, had they used him.

Self-servingly, Bentley does not mention some poor ventures that may have been at least partly his. Half a million books, for example, in the ill-fated National Library of General Knowledge were remaindered, at great loss. Other 'libraries' failed. The only 'collective' which made money for the firm (relatively small amounts in its early years) was the 'Standard Novels'.

As Bentley records, Colburn's desperate sale fell short of what was needed. Heavy loss was sustained. Whether it was, as alleged, entirely Colburn's fault may be questioned. But Bentley could legitimately claim inexperience. The cannier, older Richard Bentley (the brigand who pounced so voraciously on Dickens) would not, for example, have rejected Carlyle's *Sartor Resartus*.

By this stage, the clash of personalities had progressed beyond quarrel to outright battle. Colburn, who had kept a private office for himself throughout the partnership—first in Golden Square, then in nearby Great Marlborough Street—had by now made it his daily place of business communicating (farcically) with Bentley, in New Burlington Street (a few hundred yards away), by letter or messenger. Financial problems, and personal incompatibility, had clearly brought simmering disagreements to boiling point. There is no particular casus belli recorded, but there must have been rows and shouting matches.

It was at this point that Bentley began his lifelong anti-

Colburn campaign, talking his partner down whenever he could. Colburn was the guilty party. Taking charge, with just over one month left in the life of their three-year partnership, Bentley instructed his lawyers to compile a 'case' for judicial opinion should there be legal dispute over separation. Henry Colburn's 'disposition to be troublesome' is prominently noted, as is the fact that Bentley believed that Colburn had agreed not to sell to the trade small quantities of the titles he personally owned without his partner's permission.[211] He had not honoured that point of the original agreement. It was not a big thing, but Bentley wanted his case to depend on Colburn's continuous transgressions. The 'case' document notes that the original Indenture had made no formal provision on paper for either partner to be paid out of incoming revenue. They had struck a verbal agreement (during one of their relatively rare meetings) to pay themselves in proportion to the usual three-fifths / two-fifths ratio. (According to the Bentley obituary, Colburn took a stipendiary £75 per month and Bentley took £50.)

The 'case' also states that the annual stocktaking and ledger balancing mandated by the Indenture never took place—an amazing omission by the otherwise conscientious Bentley. But Colburn had put so much on his shoulders, he may perhaps have had no time. The upshot was that, at the end of three years, the partners had no idea whether they were in profit or in debt, or what their stock was worth, or how to go forward. Bentley suspected he was being short-changed—but how could he know? By this stage intercourse between the partners was reduced to un-partnerly lawyers' letters and frigid correspondence. It was no way to run a business.

The 'case' material was held in abeyance. Bentley intended takeover, lock stock and barrel: he was no longer a junior partner, and felt strong enough to do so.

---

[211] British Library, Add.MS.46632A, 38–43.

A new Indenture was duly drawn up preparatory to the dissolution of the partnership on 1 September 1832. This Indenture was necessary because Colburn and Bentley had failed to carry through to either partner's satisfaction the terms of the original Indenture. The new (terminal) agreement set the price of Colburn's good will at £4,000 (a significant reduction from the original £10,000) plus his three-fifths of any currently incoming profits; Bentley would buy their unpublished stock and copyrights at cost (just under £6,000); and the two would bid, item by item, for their published stock and copyrights.[212] The September 1832 Indenture sought to ensure that Colburn kept his semi-retirement status to the letter by enjoining him never to publish any new works, or open any shop, within twenty miles of London or Edinburgh, under penalty of a £5,000 fine. He was rusticated. But at least he could keep his business name 'Henry Colburn and Co.', which had a larger, longer, reputation than 'Bentley and Co.' Colburn agreed to limit his business activities but promptly ignored the 'agreement'.

It is likely that Colburn intended, or half-intended, to abide by the terms of the Indenture and go into semi-retirement and business exile. In the event—widening the small loophole the document left open—he would not. In the short term, however, he acquiesced to get the whole thing over with and move on.

On 15 September 1832, he and Bentley sent out a joint circular notifying their clients and customers of the dissolution that had occurred two weeks before. A copy of this notice is among the Bentley Papers, along with Colburn's printed cover letter, which spells out his personal position:

> The accompanying circular will inform you of my having retired from the Publishing Business, and that

---

[212] British Library, Add.MS.46632A, 57–70.

my late Partner, Mr Bentley, has succeeded to the same. It is my intention to confine myself for the future to the management of my Periodical Publications and to the disposal of my own stock of Books.[213]

Colburn, the world might apprehend, was now finished as a full-time publisher. Indeed, a publisher of any kind other than of his journals, which he retained (it would be five years before Bentley struck in with his *Miscellany* and a novelist, Dickens, whom Colburn could never aspire to, dearly as he would have liked to). If the partnership had devolved into war, Bentley was the victor.

---

[213] British Library, Add.MS.46632A, 106–107.

Alfred Croquis delt

M. Blessington

AUTHOR OF "CONVERSATIONS WITH LORD BYRON."

BREAKING THE CHAIN

Colburn went into retreat for three years. There were still, however, faint signs of life. What other than publishing books did Henry Colburn, publisher, have to live for? He was a widower, with no known family, still only fiftyish, and his health, evidently, recovered from its 1830 downturn. He had unrivalled professional expertise, a nucleus of authors and editors who liked working with him, and an archive of copyrights ('my own stock of books') to 'work', and a handful of periodicals to publish. And, of course, he still had an office in the heart of the West End, at Great Marlborough Street.

Over 1833–35 he published only thirteen titles. The few items of interest among this lean crop are the three volumes of Hood's popular *Comic Annual,* Jared Sparks's *Life and Writings of George Washington* (1834), the Countess Blessington's *Conversations with Lord Byron* (1834), and John Evelyn's *Silva* (1835). These works were published under Colburn's imprint but through Bentley: a very strange arrangement, as Sadleir points out. It clearly testifies to the Brigand of Burlington Street's desire to keep Colburn in chains.

It is clear that Colburn was at something of a loss. Many of 'his' bestselling authors were 'his' no longer, but transferred, as property, to Bentley. Furthermore, over this interim period, Colburn was constantly harassed by threatened legal action by Bentley, who hounded his former partner, ever fearful of his back-sliding from the 1832 dissolution agreement. Colburn chafed at the 'trifling' alleged infringements ('mere accidents') as he called them, and the 'few shillings' they represented.[214] An attempt to publish an anthology of past articles in the *New Monthly* was alleged, absurdly, by Bentley to be a 'new book'. It was one of a series of petty arguments.

Colburn may not have been left with much, but Bentley could not take away his resourcefulness. In March 1835, we find him running cheap editions of old novels at 4s a volume, advertised as 'adapted to county libraries'. With the arrival of railways, the connection of the metropolis and provinces was newly energized. More imaginatively, he devised what he mischievously called 'Colburn's Standard Novelists', at 6s a volume, purchasable (this was genuinely innovative) at 1s per weekly part. For this competitor to Bentley's (his alone) now booming Standard Novels, Colburn exhumed his old standbys, *Pelham, Philip Tremaine, The Disowned,* and *Brambletye House.* The content of his list is stale. What was fresh, and exciting, was the part-issue gimmick. This may well have been an inspiration for Dickens's serialization of *Pickwick Papers,* with Chapman and Hall, which also took off in 1836.[215] Bentley, predictably but unsuccessfully, attempted to kill 'Colburn's Standard Novelists' on the reasonable grounds that it infringed the brand name of what was now his series.[216] Colburn carried on with his look-alike (in name and format) series. By now Henry Colburn had created a new professional emblem: the Phoenix. The bird of rebirth.

On New Year's Day, 1835, Colburn issued a printed statement announcing that he would no longer be publishing his journals through Bentley's firm; he would undertake the

---

[214] British Library, Add.MS.59631, 7.

[215] See J. Sutherland, 'Dickens's serializing Imitators' in *Victorian Novelists, Readers and Publishers.*

[216] British Library, Add.MS.46632A, 177–189.

business himself.[217] He also announced that he would limit Bentley's exclusive rights to some of his books to a period of one month; after that, Colburn would regard himself as free to sell them from, and via, his own shop in Great Marlborough Street. Bentley preserved this announcement among his papers, presumably as ammunition for his lawyers' next assault on Colburn, but there are no records of legal action. Bentley had previously threatened legal action on the flimsiest pretexts. On this occasion, with the law clearly on his side, he failed to act. Had he lost his nerve?

Colburn had certainly not lost his. In May 1836, he sprang back on the offensive by launching a new list from Windsor. The site was one mile more than the statutory twenty miles distant and also satisfying close to royalty. Colburn would certify his fondness for the place by commissioning Harrison Ainsworth's magnificent *Windsor Castle* in 1843. His trade announcements were once again jaunty, for example: 'Mr Colburn has now opened a new and extensive Publishing Establishment at Windsor, a spot which affords peculiar advantages for an undertaking of this nature'.

It was provocative in the highest degree. Bentley, inevitably, consulted lawyers. They evidently told him not to waste his money.[218] The law, and the terminal Indenture, did not prohibit Colburn publishing 21 miles away in a town where he had an office and home. Nor could it prevent him receiving visits from authors and editors. In other words, conducting a new business.

Years later, Bentley's grandson recalled his grandfather (for whom it was clearly a lifelong source of resentment) saying:

> I had a consultation with Mr. Knight-Bruce, and when
> I found my agreement was of no use in protecting me,
> I was exceedingly angry with Gregory (the solicitor who

---

[217] British Library, Add.MS.46632B, 1.

[218] British Library, Add.MS.46632B, 91–92.

drew it up). On this Mr. Knight-Bruce stopped me, and said I was wrong in finding fault with Mr. Gregory, and that it was impossible to frame any agreement for such a man.[219]

Knight-Bruce inquired if Colburn had offered Bentley any money to release him from the Indenture. Upon learning he had, but that Bentley was too proud to consider such a thing, Knight-Bruce's considered advice was: 'For God's sake, sir, take his money! Take his money!' Which, in the end, Bentley did. Capitulation.

On 4 June 1836, the two men signed an Agreement resolving the outstanding financial matters between them and setting the price of Colburn's freedom at £3,500.[220] One week later, Colburn handed over the money and both men signed a formal Deed of Release.[221] They also signed a strange little declaration:

> At the suggestion of our mutual Professional Friends for the better restoring harmony and good feeling between us we now withdraw all offensive representations which in the heat of a contest upon topics of difference that unfortunately arose between us, we may have been induced to make the one against the other. Dated this 11th day of June 1836.[222]

Humbug, of course. The battle between the two men, taking the form of guerilla warfare, would continue for as long as Colburn published books—something he did virtually till the day he died.

---

[219] British Library, Add.MS.46632B, 91.

[220] British Library, Add.MS.46632B, 140–141.

[221] British Library, Add.MS.46632B, 142–154.

[222] British Library, Add.MS.46632B, 155.

INDEPENDENCE REGAINED

In June 1836, Colburn ('Prometheus Unbound') was again a London publisher, established at 13 Great Marlborough Street, in his beloved West End. All his contacts were still warm. The Prince of Puffers returned to his stamping ground with all his old zest. The *Athenaeum* could not refrain from a sarcastic welcome, on 2 July: 'Mr Colburn has recommenced publishing and there is not a vacant corner in the papers or a foot of honest wall within the bills of mortality'. The problem, though, was what to advertise? The bulk of Colburn's authors were now signed over to Bentley or with Colburn's other warmed viper in his bosom, Saunders (of Saunders and Otley). Colburn did as best he could with the loyal and indefatigably productive Mrs. Gore who, in 1836, turned out for him one of her finest silver-fork narratives, *Mrs Armytage* and the less admirable *Diary of a Désennuyée*. Together with Lady Malet's *Violet: or the Danseuse* (a favourite novel of Colburn's) and *La Duchesse de la Vallière,* by his old prima donna, Madame de Genlis, Colburn had a respectably glittering show of fashionable books. But with only a dozen new titles, his output for 1836 was slender.

In 1837 things picked up with twenty-three titles, including Disraeli's bestselling *Henrietta Temple* and *Venetia,* Marryat's *Snarleyyow,* Galt's *Life of Byron,* Mrs. S. C. Hall's *Uncle Horace,* a bundle of three silver-fork novels by Mrs. Gore and two by Lady Bury. Although his output was never again to reach 1828–30 proportions, Colburn averaged around fifteen titles a year for the rest of his publishing career.

Over the decade after the split, Colburn devoted himself to a life and death struggle with Bentley. The two men's feuding, poaching, copycatting and upstaging of each other was a spectacle richly comic to contemporaries. A large number of popular authors bounced between the two houses, playing one publisher off against another for better bids. On the whole, Bentley had the better of this kind of struggle. He had more money behind him, was the younger man, and had inherited (purchased) Colburn's publishing business in running order. Undoubtedly, too, he benefited from being thought the more honest of the two. It must have been double-distilled gall to Colburn when Bentley was named Publisher in Ordinary to the King in 1833. That trumped publishing from Royal Windsor any day of the week.

OLD PUBLISHER, YOUNG ENGLAND

Colburn's relationship with Disraeli—his most lustrous author—endured throughout all the upsets and storms of the partnership. The friendship between the two men was solid, even though it pleased Disraeli privately to refer to Colburn as the publishing world's Artful Dodger—the lovable Dickensian rogue. Disraeli knew his publisher through and through, the good and the bad, but never forgot who had given him help in his youth. When Disraeli was awarded an earldom in 1876, he was granted his request to become 'Earl of Beaconsfield', a title he had invented fifty years before in his first Colburn publication, *Vivian Grey*.

The trust between publisher and author was most gloriously demonstrated by what posterity has seen as Colburn's finest crop of fiction—Disraeli's 'Young England' novels—a trilogy which would change the whole climate of British politics, to this day. For the first time, Disraeli—now a rising young politician—permitted his name to be printed on the title pages of *Coningsby* (1844), Sybil (1845) and *Tancred* (1847).

The Young England ethos, as its name implies, rejuvenated old Toryism, while retaining its core essence, as most recently promulgated by Peel. The main Disraelian tenet was that feudalism represented the high point in British historical greatness. The Young Englanders particularly disdained the revolution of 1688 (the so-called 'Dutch Settlement'). Young England condemned utilitarianism, supported Bolingbroke, Puseyism, and the New Tracts. Their 'Bible' was Digby's *The Broad Stone of Honour, Or the True Sense and Practice of Chivalry* (1822).

'One Nation' Toryism—a clarion call through the subsequent ages—was formulated in these three novels. *Sybil: Or the Two Nations* is the most read and reprinted of the trilogy. The binational gulf between rich and poor is, if anything, wider today than it was in 1845. But, for the discriminating reader, *Coningsby* is the most interesting, and ultimately formative, of the three. A summary reveals the power of Disraeli's thought, and the veins of absurdity which run through it.

Harry Coningsby's parents marry against the wishes of his father, Lord Monmouth. Later orphaned, Harry regains his grandfather's favour and is sent to Eton. There he saves the life of Oswald Millbank (an industrialist's son, based on Gladstone) who becomes a lifelong friend.

Coningsby leaves Eton for Cambridge (all this, of course, in Disraeli's dreams—though, like Coningsby, he did marry for money). Cambridge does its best but the main educational influence in his life comes from a chance meeting in a thunderstorm with the mysterious and omnicompetent Jew, Sidonia.

Sidonia inspires Harry with new Conservative idealism and the young man falls out with his grandfather when he offers him an 'agreeably safe' seat (i.e., from a rotten borough) in Parliament. On the Marquis, his grandfather's death, Harry finds himself disinherited. But he sets himself to work as a barrister, eventually wins the patronage of the industrialist Millbank and successfully enters the House of Commons. He comes into huge wealth when Monmouth's illegitimate daughter dies, leaving him her fortune. Harry marries Edith Millbank, symbolizing the happy union of old rank and new money.

The novel made a huge impact. It inspired an anonymous squib, *The Anti-Coningsby* (1844) and Thackeray's deadly burlesque, *Codlingsby* (1847, see below). There were a number of 'keys' supplied, informing the general public whom the dramatis personae were based on. Disraeli / Coningsby topped the list.

Meanwhile, Colburn's feud with Bentley festered on, spluttering like a saucepan of overheated porridge, to the amusement of the London book trade. There was one particularly bad-tempered spat with Disraeli at its centre. In 1845, latching on to the éclat of the Young England novels, Bentley brought out *The Young Duke* (no mystery now about the author) in his Standard Novels series. Disraeli and Colburn were furious, disputing ownership of the copyright. If there was any work which was quintessentially Colburn it was *The Young Duke*. Bentley, after a year's quarrelling, won the point. There was some underhand dealing. At one point Bentley said he would cede ownership of *The Young Duke* if, in compensation, Disraeli offered him a new work of fiction. Disraeli refused. He was Colburn's man and would not desert him. This lifelong loyalty (to both men's credit) was confirmed, when shortly before his retirement, Disraeli gave Colburn and Co. a major non-fiction work, the 'political biography' of his parliamentary ally, Lord George Bentinck. Other publishers were queuing up to get the work—but Disraeli put it his old 'venerable' friend's way, even though he must have known he was easing, gracefully, out of business.

When that happened, for the few years of his life which remained, Disraeli—very much a great man nowadays—maintained the friendship, dining at the Colburns' house in fashionable Bryanston Square.[223] There was a residual interest in reprints. Colburn's chosen successors Daniel Hurst and Henry Blackett continued the care of Disraeli's literary properties. They were eventually sold back by Colburn to Disraeli—collective reprints in prospect—for the token price of £200.

---

[223] Renton 237.

After Colburn died on 16 August 1855, Richard Bentley pounced. On 1 February 1856, he wrote to Disraeli:

> Hearing from various quarters that you are engaged upon a Life of Bolingbroke, I write to ask you to do me the favor of permitting me to negociate with you for the copyright of that work. So long as Mr Colburn survived, I did not approach you with any offers, but now, perhaps, you will allow me to say, that it will give me pleasure to have an opportunity of becoming your publisher. Whatever may be the consideration agreed upon, in the event of an arrangement being made, I beg to say it would be made, as I do always now, in cash.[224]

The last sentence was pure Bentley. What Disraeli replied has not survived. But he did not rise to the bait.

The high point of the Disraeli-Colburn partnership (much more substantial than that between Colburn and Bentley) had been the 'Young England' trilogy. But for all the success, and lasting impact, of these novels, Colburn's interest in the 'hungry forties', free trade, Chartism and one-nation Conservatism was evidently slight. Political strong meat was not to his taste. While the loyalty of Disraeli was a major comfort to Colburn, the Disraeli of *The Young Duke* was more his line of fiction.

---

[224] Hughenden Papers, 235/4, 91.

Harriet Martineau.

AUTHOR OF "ILLUSTRATIONS OF POLITICAL ECONOMY."

COLBURN'S MARRIED LADIES

The nucleus of Colburn's list was provided by a trio of married women writers: Mrs. Gore, Mrs. Frances Trollope, and Mrs. Marsh. Between them they turned in some fifty three-deckers for Colburn. Enough, en masse, to crush any lover of silver-fork to happy extinction. It was family or marital crisis which drove all three of these women to their voluminous careers in fiction. They were well paid. Mrs. Trollope, for instance, had a normal fee of 800 guineas after the success of *Hargrave* in 1843. Not that Colburn's relationship with these ladies was always tranquil. In the same year, 1843, he almost went to court with Mrs. Trollope, over disputed payments.

Of the three, Mrs. Marsh (who produced regularly from 1846) is the most underrated today. Her fiction typically represented Colburn's reluctant adaptation to the domestic mode of fiction preferred by mid-Victorians. The high life of the Regency was a thing of the past. Mrs. Marsh (1791–1874) could remember it. She had been born Sara Anne Caldwell into the landed gentry: her father was a Deputy Lieutenant of Staffordshire, her mother an heiress. She married a banker, Arthur Marsh, in 1817. He was ruined, seven years later, by the notorious swindler, Henry Fauntleroy. His crime and punishment (the rope) would inspire some Newgate fiction.

Encouraged by Harriet Martineau (who introduced her to Colburn), Marsh began publishing fiction in 1834.

Like Martineau, her work is earnest. And it was popular enough to put bread on the family table. Arthur died in 1849, leaving his wife with seven children to provide for. As a widow Mrs. Marsh wrote to support herself—which she did comfortably, beginning her trademark style of narrative with *Lettice Arnold* (1850). In 1858, her brother and she inherited the family estate, changing her name to Marsh-Caldwell. It was the kind of thing that happened more in romantic fiction than in life, but it did happen to her.

The quality of her fiction is serenely dull. The most interesting of her works in *Emilia Wyndham* (1846), whose heroine has to cope after her father is swindled out of his property. The plot draws, patently, on her husband's financial misfortunes. The novel, popular in its day, remains highly readable and totally neglected by posterity. The curse of Colburn.

Mrs. Trollope (with a career total of 35 titles) turned to fiction with the bankruptcy of her lawyer husband (a man teetering on the brink of suicide). Of her seven children all but two (the novelists Anthony and Thomas Adolphus) died before their mother. She was loyal to Colburn although her best novel, *The Vicar of Wrexhill* (1837), came out under Bentley's imprint.

Mrs. Gore (1799–1861) was one of the most prolific, and underrated, novelists of the century. She was, incontrovertibly, one of the most facile practitioners of fashionable fiction. Two of her finest novels, *Greville* and *Cecil,* were published in the same week in 1841—keenly competing with each other (she and Colburn used anonymity to hide the fact).

She was born Catherine Grace Frances Moody. Her father was a Nottinghamshire wine merchant. At an early age she showed literary skills and her family nicknamed her 'The Poetess'. In 1823, she married Captain Charles Arthur Gore, of the Life Guards. Although he left the service in the same year, she evidently saw some of the high life she was to describe so vividly. She herself claimed, in her preface to *Pin Money* (1831), that she was transferring 'the familiar narrative of Miss Austen to a higher sphere of society'. George IV was an admirer. Her work was puffed, outrageously, by Colburn.

For reasons which are not clear (almost certainly debt or scandal), she moved to France in the early 1830s, living, thereafter, a life of social seclusion. She had ten children. Her later fiction, in keeping with the times, is more moral and domestic. At the end of her life, she was blind. Of her ten children, only two survived her. After a heroically long writing career, she inherited a substantial property in 1850. But she was impoverished, five years later, when her former guardian, Sir John Dean Paul, defrauded her of £20,000. She died, exhausted, at the age of sixty-one. On such sadness was the glittering structure of fashionable fiction built.

COLBURN'S MARRIED LADY: AT HOME IN BRYANSTON SQUARE

One knows tantalizingly little about Colburn's private life—one suspects that, outside the world of books, he barely had one. But documentation, and subsequent references, record that he remarried.

On 26 February 1841, he signed a marriage licence allegation at the Faculty Office in preparation for a union between himself and Eliza Ann Crosbie, 'a spinster'. The date of the actual marriage ceremony is not known but may be presumed to have taken place shortly thereafter in the couple's parish church of St. James's, Westminster.

A number of sources—principally Colburn's obituaries—refer to Eliza as the only daughter of Captain Robert Crosbie, R.N. The marriage licence allegation states, according to the usual formula, that Eliza had reached the age of at least twenty-one years. What little we know of Miss Crosbie / Mrs. Colburn derives from her second marriage, in 1856, as a very new widow to John Forster—Dickens's closest friend, confidant, and biographer. There is some question of Eliza's age. Dickens estimated her, at the time of marriage, at 'five or six and thirty', giving a birth date of around 1820.[225] This would mean that she was in fact barely twenty-one years old at the time of her marriage

---

[225] Dickens, *Letters*, VIII, 165.

to Colburn, when he was fifty-seven. How the couple met and what effect the vast age difference had on their marriage are questions that Dickens does not answer. He does, however, reveal that Eliza had a speech impediment; in a letter written in 1860, he quotes the then Mrs. Forster as speaking of 'brilgil up the Lord Chief Barrel's youlgest childrel to see the Lord Mayor's Show.'[226] In this same letter and in others, however, Dickens also discloses that despite her speech impediments, Mrs. Forster was talkative. He concedes, however, that she was 'agreeable, and rather pretty'.[227] S. C. Hall, an intimate friend of Colburn, referred to Eliza as 'an estimable lady'.[228] The younger Richard Renton goes further: '[Colburn's] wife was, I think, the most charming, the sweetest-natured woman it is possible to conceive. Petite, dainty in form and feature, she was, at the same time, clever and shrewd beyond the average woman of her day'.[229] Like Dickens and Hall, Renton spoke from personal acquaintance. She paid visits to his mother when he was a lad and brought him Christmas presents. The Colburns, the evidence suggests, were a sociable couple and entertained distinguished company at 14 Bryanston Square, where they had moved in 1852. Disraeli, Leigh Hunt, and Dickens ate at their table. Colburn had evidently retired comfortably funded. Dickens commented on the fine paintings (notably by Daniel Maclise—who did one of the finest portraits of Dickens himself) on the Colburns' walls.

---

[226] Dickens, *Letters,* IX, 339.

[227] Dickens, *Letters* VIII, 165.

[228] Hall, op cit., I, 316.

[229] Renton, p. 94.

AUTHOR OF "ILLUSTRATIONS OF TIME".

LOSING THE BATTLE

After Henry Colburn's return to publishing, he amassed a list that was solid and intermittently impressive, but he had no answer to the superstars that Bentley gradually recruited to his imprint in the late 1830s with Dickens and Ainsworth. Colburn's attempt to cap these exciting young writers' successive editorship of the all-conquering *Bentley's Miscellany* by recruiting (the aged) Frederick Marryat as exclusive contributor and the appointment of Theodore Hook as editor of the *New Monthly* (additionally subtitled '... *and Humorist*') was a flop. Not least because Hook was on his last legs and died in 1841. Colburn's attempt to have Mrs. Trollope match *Oliver Twist* with *Michael Armstrong* was a gallant failure. Nor could Colburn find an illustrator to match Cruikshank. He did eventually net Ainsworth as editor of the *New Monthly*, but this was merely a prelude to selling him the magazine (for £2,500) in 1845.

Between 1840 and 1852, Colburn is listed as having 321 new titles, of which 194 are fiction, 44 memoirs or history, and 56 works of travel literature. A few merit naming. In 1840, three years after Victoria's accession, Colburn made his most appreciated genuflection (of many) with the Misses Stricklands' (Elizabeth and Agnes) *Lives of the Queens of England*. The series was a success for its publisher, critically and financially. He grudgingly paid the 'unbusinesslike' authors £2,000 for the entire copyright. After Colburn's death, in 1855, it was valued at £6,900 and

Miss Strickland finally recovered it from Mrs. John Forster (the former Mrs. Colburn) for £1,862 in 1863. In death, as in life, Colburn could, on occasion, be a hard publisher for authors to deal with. In 1844, there appeared Colburn's most distinguished travel book, Warburton's *The Crescent and the Cross*.

In 1845, Colburn took a risk with the Rev. Richard Cobbold's *History of Margaret Catchpole,* paying the clergyman and amateur novelist £600 for his semi-documentary, rattling tale of Suffolk life and smuggling at the turn of the nineteenth century. Unusually for a three decker, the novel carried illustrations by its author. The heroine is a farm labourer's daughter who goes into service. She has two lovers: the dashing smuggler, Will Laud, and the solid countryman, John Barry. In the climax of the novel, Margaret steals a horse to ride to London and marry Will. But she is caught, sentenced to death, then reprieved. She later escapes, daringly, from Ipswich gaol and, in a bloody shootout, in which Laud is killed, she is recaptured. After ten years as a transported convict in Australia, Margaret returns to Suffolk, to marry John and end life as a respectable matron. The author's mother knew the original 'Margaret' and helped her to that respectability. Colburn made a good decision in buying the work.

He was similarly keen-witted in publishing Catherine Crowe's popular *The Story of Lilly Dawson* (1847). Its heroine is shipwrecked as a girl, forcibly adopted by smugglers and forced to be 'everybody's servant, and maid of all work in the most emphatic sense of the term'. Prostituted, that is. Her Cinderella-like return to wealthy, middle-class existence is fraught with difficulties. At the end of her adventures, she disdains gentility and returns to marry a lover, Philip, from the lower orders. The last sentence of the novel informs the reader that she died happy, and 'at peace with God and Man'. These two novels mark a very distant departure from 'fashionability'.

Colburn's imprint is on the best of Ainsworth's historical romances, *Windsor Castle* (1843). To his credit, Colburn helped launch the careers of some worthy young novelists in the 1840s and early 1850s. They include Anthony Trollope (*The Kellys and the O'Kellys*, 1849; *La Vendée*, 1850), Margaret Oliphant (*Passages in the Life of Mrs Margaret Maitland*, 1849—a work praised by Charlotte Brontë and the first of her more than 100 novels)—and R. S. Surtees (*Handley Cross*, 1843). In this middle part of Surtees' 'Jorrocks' trilogy, John Jorrocks, a vulgar, twenty-stone cockney, enriched by greengrocery (in London) becomes master of the Handley Cross hunt. Jollity ensues. And Colburn was Charles Lever's first English publisher, in 1844, with *Arthur O'Leary* (illustrated by George Cruikshank). The subtitle, 'His Wanderings and Ponderings in Many Lands' indicates the novel's (characteristic) loosely strung narrative.

This is not an outstanding roll of honour compared, for example, to what could be cited for Chapman and Hall, or Blackwood's (or, perish the thought, Bentley) over the same period. But it is not negligible and comprehensively belies Sadleir's contemptuous 'perhaps four copyrights of lasting value'.

BACON AND BUNGAY

If you wish to keep your reputation in good shape it is wise not to pick a fight with the greatest satirist of your time—which is what Colburn did (dragging with him Richard Bentley into the line of satirical fire).

Thackeray, 'writing for his life' as a jobbing (anonymous or pseudonymous) penny-a-liner, had been writing for Colburn's *New Monthly* since 1838. In the early 1840s, with the great anniversary coming up, he resolved to write a 'Waterloo Novel'. It would be, by his standards, a major work. He had a lot invested in it.

He sent what was provisionally called 'A Novel without a Hero' (a little anti-Carlylean joke), alias 'Pen and Pencil Sketches of English Society' to Colburn. The 'Vanity Fair' title came to Thackeray, while sleeping, shortly before the novel was published. All three titles are on the novel's published frontispieces.

Colburn may not have been the first publisher Thackeray tried out in (probably) late 1844. The idea was that the novel would be serialized in the *New Monthly*. What Colburn would have seen was epistolary narrative (parts of which would ultimately resurface in chapters 8 and 9 of *Vanity Fair*).

Colburn evidently accepted the proposed 'Novel without a Hero' sample at a standard £1 per printed page. Hardly magnum opus remuneration, but reflecting Thackeray's growing reputation as something more than a mere penny a liner. A pound a pager was up the scale.

The completed work, had Thackeray been allowed to complete it according to its original conception, would have been shorter than the *Vanity Fair* we have, and pictureless. Colburn was evidently in no hurry. It seems that some token amount of money changed hands.

Thackeray evidently intended to get round to writing his 'Novel without a Hero' in the anniversary year, 1845. Preparatory to that, he made a trip to the field of Waterloo. 'Let an Englishman go to that field', he wrote in an article for *Fraser's*, 'and he *never forgets it*'. Nor did Thackeray, it would emerge, ever forget a grudge.

Colburn's fortunes were at a low ebb in the mid-1840s and required some nimble footwork on his part. He was looking for someone to take over the *New Monthly*. Thackeray (who had editorial experience) may well have been thought a contender—but he had insufficient capital. His marriage was under huge stress (his wife having lost her mind). The arrangement for the proto-*Vanity Fair* came to nothing when, in June 1845, Colburn sold the *New Monthly*, lock stock and barrel, to another historical novelist, whose star had risen higher than Thackeray's, W. H. Ainsworth.

William Harrison Ainsworth did not like Thackeray one little bit. He (Thackeray) had mercilessly satirized Ainsworth's 'Newgate' (i.e., crime-glorifying) novels, *Rookwood* and *Jack Sheppard* in *Fraser's Magazine*. People were still laughing.

Thackeray was brusquely informed that under the new management of the *New Monthly Magazine*, his 'Novel without a Hero' was no longer required. He was hurt. And Thackeray was not a writer you could hurt with impunity. Ainsworth (by far the stupider man) gave him an opportunity for revenge. On taking over the *New Monthly*, in June 1845, Ainsworth, in a calculated snub to Thackeray, one guesses, advertised the fact that, henceforth, its pages would be graced by novels 'by eminent hands'. Eminence did not, self-evidently, include the cockney 'Michael

Angelo Titmarsh' *sobriquet* Thackeray most commonly wrote under. Or its creator.

On 5 July 1845, Thackeray hit back with a squib in *Punch* about 'eminent hands' and, most vituperatively, a burlesque series of the funniest fictional parodies in the annals of English literature, 'Novels by Eminent Hands'. It ran in *Punch* from April to October 1847. By this time, after much hawking around, Thackeray had found a publisher, Bradbury and Evans, for the novel Colburn and Ainsworth had accepted and then rejected.

The parodies were, every one of them, of a 'name' Colburn author:

1. *George De Barnwell,* by Sir E. L. B. L., Bart. [Edward Lytton Bulwer Lytton]
2. *Codlingsby,* by D. Shrewsberry, Esq. [Disraeli]
3. *Phil Fogarty.* A Tale of The Fighting Onety-Oneth. by Harry Rollicker. [Charles Lever]
4. *Barbazure.* by G. P. R. Jeames, Esq., etc. [G.P.R. James]
5. *Lords and Liveries.* by the Authoress of "Dukes and Dejeuners," "Hearts and Diamonds," "Marchionesses and Milliners," etc. etc. [Mrs. Gore]
6. *Crinoline.* by Je-mes Pl-sh, Esq. [Disraeli, again]
7. *The Stars and Stripes.* the Author of "The Last of the Mulligans," "Pilot," etc. [James Fenimore Cooper]

'Codlingsby', the spoof of *Coningsby* (published a few months earlier), is the cruelest of the bunch and outright anti-Semitic:

> The Talmud relates that Adam had two wives—Zillah the dark beauty; Eva the fair one. The ringlets of Zillah were black; those of Eva were golden. The eyes of Zillah were night; those of Eva were morning. Codlingsby was fair—of the fair Saxon race of Hengist and Horsa—they called him Miss Codlingsby at school; but how much fairer was Miriam the Hebrew!

Her hair had that deep glowing tinge in it which has been the delight of all painters, and which, therefore, the vulgar sneer at. It was of burning auburn. Meandering over her fairest shoulders in twenty thousand minute ringlets, it hung to her waist and below it. A light blue velvet fillet clasped with a diamond aigrette (valued at two hundred thousand tomauns, and bought from Lieutenant Vicovich, who had received it from Dost Mahomed), with a simple bird of paradise, formed her head-gear. A sea-green cymar with short sleeves, displayed her exquisitely moulded arms to perfection, and was fastened by a girdle of emeralds over a yellow satin frock. Pink gauze trousers spangled with silver, and slippers of the same color as the band which clasped her ringlets (but so covered with pearls that the original hue of the charming little papoosh disappeared entirely) completed her costume. She had three necklaces on, each of which would have dowered a Princess—her fingers glistened with rings to their rosy tips, and priceless bracelets, bangles, and armlets wound round an arm that was whiter than the ivory grand piano on which it leaned.

Colburn and Ainsworth must have writhed as London laughed. Disraeli and Lytton never forgave Thackeray (and Disraeli, long after Thackeray's death, returned the satire in *Endymion,* with the novelist 'St Barbe'). G.P.R. James changed his 'two horsemen' openings, about which Thackeray was hilarious. Mrs. Gore's treatment was the most affectionate (Thackeray admired her, on her best days). Cooper was wholly indifferent. 'Last of the Mulligans' is good, though.

Thackeray had not finished—at least, not with Colburn. Following *Vanity Fair,* the novel that propelled him to the top of the tree with Dickens, he wrote a bildungsroman, *Pendennis,* which featured an extended subplot dealing, satirically, with the London literary 'Grub Street' which he,

Thackeray, had now risen above. Arthur Pendennis, the hero, writes a silver-fork novel. It brings him into contact with two of Grub Street's grubbiest denizens, Bacon and Bungay. Warrington, Arthur's adviser on things literary, fills him in as to these publishers, both of whom are interested in acquiring Arthur's *Walter Lorraine*:

> 'Bungay and Bacon are at daggers drawn; each married the sister of the other, and they were for some time the closest friends and partners. Hack says it was Mrs. Bungay who caused all the mischief between the two; whereas Shandon, who reads for Bungay a good deal, says Mrs. Bacon did the business; but I don't know which is right, Peachum or Lockit. But since they have separated, it is a furious war between the two publishers; and no sooner does one bring out a book of travels, or poems, a magazine or periodical, quarterly, or monthly, or weekly, or annual, but the rival is in the field with something similar. I have heard poor Shandon tell with great glee how he made Bungay give a grand dinner at Blackwall to all his writers, by saying that Bacon had invited his corps to an entertainment at Greenwich. When Bungay engaged your celebrated friend Mr. Wagg to edit the 'Londoner,' Bacon straightway rushed off and secured Mr. Grindle to give his name to the 'Westminster Magazine.' When Bacon brought out his comic Irish novel of 'Barney Brallaghan,' off went Bungay to Dublin, and produced his rollicking Hibernian story of 'Looney MacTwolter.' When Doctor Hicks brought out his 'Wanderings in Mesopotamia' under Bacon's auspices, Bungay produced Professor Sandiman's 'Researches in Zahara;' and Bungay is publishing his 'Pall Mall Gazette' as a counterpoise to Bacon's 'Whitehall Review.'

'Wagg' is generally taken to be Theodore Hook. 'Marmaduke' Bungay, of course, is taken to be Colburn. It must certainly have been so taken by Colburn himself.

Describing the offices of the two warring publishers, Thackeray makes the identification clear by allusion to the two authors Colburn could be proudest about, and doubtless boasted about:

> Exactly opposite to Bacon's house was that of Mr. Bungay, which was newly painted and elaborately decorated in the style of the seventeenth century, so that you might have fancied stately Mr. Evelyn passing over the threshold, or curious Mr. Pepys examining the books in the window.[230]

Thackeray was up with all the literary gossip and one wonders whether Colburn's marriage, formed at the time he was entering into partnership with Bentley, was a factor in the break-up. The shreds of evidence identify the first Mrs. Colburn as a crockery-throwing termagant with a weakness for the bottle. Perhaps she did come between the partners somehow.

Thackeray's satire stamped, indelibly, the Bacon and Bungay caricature on the two rivalrous publishers. They were, thereafter, not Henry Colburn or Richard Bentley, but Bacon and Bungay. Figures of fun. Bentley, with a longer run into the late nineteenth century, was less wounded than his former partner.

---

[230] Ch. XXXI, p. 399.

WINDING UP

The last year of Colburn's trading, 1852, found him in better shape than any period since the late 1820s. Examining the twenty-four books listed in his last business year, one is struck by how closely the mixture matches that of forty years earlier. Colburn still builds on the tripod of popular fiction (fifteen titles, now rather domestic than fashionable), travels (five titles) and memoirs of interesting people (four titles). The three-decker remains his main shop-window display (there are thirteen in his 1852 list).

Since the break-up with Bentley in the 1830s, Colburn had amassed a powerful backlist. His advertisements are a judicious mixture of established non-fiction ('Interesting Works', as they are called) and novels of the day. Colburn was a famous hoarder of copyrights and stock. It is fascinating to see him in 1852 remaindering two-volume sets of *Violet: or the Danseuse,* printed almost twenty years before.

The jewel (refurbished) in Colburn's list for 1852–53 is the new edition of Evelyn's *Diary,* now complete in four volumes. It partners the enlarged version of Pepys, issued in 1848. The Stricklands' *Lives of the Queens of England* (finished in 1848) was reissued in eight volumes at 4 guineas. Unable to resist cheapening his own wares, Colburn also put out a pot-boiling *Lives of the Princesses of England,* by Mrs. Everett Green (4 vols at 10/6 apiece). Disraeli's *Political Biography of Lord George Bentinck* was in its fourth edition by 1 February (1 vol, 10/6d). *The Crescent and the Cross* was in a ninth edition, at 10/6d.

Colburn, for all his advanced years (he must, by now, have been in his seventies) was clearly feeling expansive. The whole field of general trade publishing was booming in 1852. It was soon to hit a recession with Crimean War. But Colburn, lucky as ever, escaped a crisis which, to his pleasure, one imagines, came near to destroying Bentley.

It was a propitious time to sell and Colburn did so. As he had in 1825, he incorporated himself as 'Henry Colburn & Co.' just before doing so. In January 1853 (Colburn's secession was gradual), the business at 13 Great Marlborough Street was taken over by one of Colburn's assistants, Daniel Hurst (1826–71), in partnership with Henry Blackett (1803–70), a much older man, who apparently put up the cash. Hurst supplied the energy. These two, his chosen heirs, continued the firm's activity in established Colburnian style and became renowned as publishers of romantic three-deckers for the woman reader.

SHORT RETIREMENT: DEATH AND LEGACY

Henry Colburn was not to enjoy a long retirement. He died at his home in Bryanston Square on Thursday, 16 August 1855, at the (presumable) age of seventy-one. In his unpublished obituary of Colburn, Richard Bentley reports that his former partner had 'suffered more than a year before from a fistula, which had been operated upon by Brodie; but about a month ago the disease returned, and after three days' intense suffering he sank under it.'

Bentley attended the funeral which took place on 23 August in All Souls' Cemetery at Kensal Green. It was, he recalled, 'conducted with more than ordinary form. Hearse with four horses, and two mourning coaches, and four private carriages. The coffin had gilt trappings'. Despite this pomp, the gravestone was simple: a plain landing stone marked with the plot number [12644] and a bleak inscription: "HENRY COLBURN Died 16th August 1855"'. Even in death he contrived to keep his date of birth secret.

Eliza Colburn lost no time in proving her husband's will, wrapping up on 1 September 1855, just one week after his funeral. His death, not unexpected, was well prepared for. As the Victorian slang phrase would put it, 'he cut up well'—although details are slightly fuzzy. Colburn's obituary in the *Gentleman's Magazine* records that his estate was 'sworn to be under 35,000l.'[231] This is

---

[231] P. 548.

repeated in Curwen's *History of Booksellers*. Dickens, who had private access to Colburn's affairs (via John Forster), a year after Colburn's death, estimated that Eliza had 'as many thousand pounds as she is years of age', namely, 'five or six and thirty'.[232] This notion that she had inherited an estate worth £35,000, not under that amount, is taken up by the *Dictionary of National Biography*.[233]

As he had when parting with Bentley, Colburn, on disposing of his business to Hurst and Blackett, had kept for himself a number of valuable copyrights, and a quantity of stock. This nest-egg included *The Cross and the Crescent*, the Evelyn and Pepys diaries, Burke's *Peerage*, and *The Lives of the Queens of England*. With Dickens acting as umpire, or trustee, Colburn's copyright and stock were sold by auction on 26 May 1857. The lots fetched in excess of £14,000. Among other material, Forster acquired for himself the manuscript correspondence of Garrick, the Burke copyright, and for his wife (as investment, presumably) the Strickland copyright. The fact of the auction might suggest that Colburn's will somehow obstructed a direct transfer of property from Mrs. Colburn to her new husband.

Eliza Colburn was young, judged attractive, and wealthy. She could expect to remarry. Henry had, apparently, foreseen this and did not like the idea of merry widowhood. Richard Bentley, recorded in his diary that 'poor Colburn … was most desirous that his widow should not marry again'.[234]

It is possible that John Forster was made not quite an executor but a trustee of Colburn's estate. He had grown close to the Colburns over his years' editing Evelyn's diaries. He would become even closer. On 24 September 1856, to the astonishment of his friends (notably Dickens), John Forster married Colburn's widow. Forster, who could have told us much, has left no comment on Colburn

---

[232] *Letters*, VIII, 165.

[233] P. 49.

[234] 31 July 1860.

in voluminous writings.

The marriage was a subject of book-world gossip (as had been, fifteen years earlier, one guesses, the marriage between Eliza and Henry). According to Renton, they 'had always been the best of friends: her respect and admiration for the big, burly Northumbrian man of letters, being unbounded'.[235] Nonetheless, when Forster confided his intentions to two of his closest friends, Dickens and Bulwer Lytton, both were, reportedly, astounded. As Dickens hyperbolically put it: 'It is a thing of that kind, that after I knew it (from himself) this morning, I lay down flat, as if an Engine and Tender had fallen upon me'.[236] Forster was forty-four and a confirmed bachelor. Not, one would have supposed, a marrying kind of man.

Once married, Forster was described as 'a despot in his own house'.[237] Bentley, writing in his diary a few years into the marriage, concurred: 'Long ago no doubt the poor woman has discovered her mistake. Whatever faults Colburn might have had he was a gentleman as regards ladies and was capable on occasion of doing many kind and generous actions. Forster is a brute'.[238]

Two years later, Bentley heard that Forster was cutting old acquaintances since acquiring the money and status of 'the foolish young widow of Colburn … he can never come within a hundred miles of the character of a gentleman, a boisterous, brutal ruffian as he is'.[239] Bentley did not like Colburn—but he positively hated Forster. Forster died in 1876, seven years after finishing the great biography of Dickens which has immortalized his name. Eliza lived on until 1894. The couple are buried, side by side, in Kensal Green Cemetery (plot number 21356).

---

[235] P. 95.

[236] Dickens, *Letters,* VIII, 70.

[237] Renton, p. 114.

[238] 31 July 1860.

[239] 6 Feb. 1862.

BIBLIOMETRIC CONCLUSION: WHAT THE NUMBERS TELL US

Henry Colburn was in business from 1806 to 1853 and, according to a sifting of the *English Catalogue,* produced some 996 new titles over the period. His career was a thing of ups and downs, but if nothing else, he displayed remarkable talents for survival; all the more remarkable given his individualistic and high-risk publishing style.

The subtotals reveal Colburn to have been predominantly a producer of fiction. Of the 996, 527 are novels and stories. Of these, no fewer than 394 are three-deckers. This is the more strikingly put in proportion to the measly 29 poetry titles that his firm is listed as having published in forty-seven years' trading. As has been noted, Colburn was not, however, a mass producer of fiction before 1822. The bulk of his three-deckers (367) were published after 1825, and a disproportionate number (137) in his seven best years, from 1826–32.

Colburn was clearly influential in the 1820s in fixing the standard first-form issue for fiction as the three-volume, absurdly priced 31/6d novel, designed for exclusive sale to libraries rather than direct to the reading public. His first twenty years in fashionable West End circulating libraries helped form this preference.

Colburn's publishing personality was stamped, indelibly it seems, in the Regency. Overall, his career represents a successful adaptation of Regency ways to an increasingly industrialized Victorian book world. He seems to have appreciated the commercial fact, still evident today, that as a business, British publishing can prosper very well with old-fashioned practices. Colburn, up to his last years of trading, put out multi-volume, high-priced items for the West End carriage trade. He utterly disdained, and evidently lost nothing by disdaining, the cheap book markets opened by Charles Knight in the 1830s and Routledge in the 1850s. Colburn banked on the middle-class library reader. That class of reader would go on to dominate the British reading public (latterly via the state prescribed 'public libraries') for a century or more.

The statistics confirm Colburn as primarily a producer of small edition, high-price books. 522 of his 996 books cost £1 or more. 292 cost 30s or more (but only 54 more than £2). The bulk of Colburn's cheap books came out before 1822. There were 115 costing £1 or less, out of a total output of 178 in the period 1806–22, when he was starting up in business life. By contrast there were only 65 books costing £1 or less in the period 1837–52 out of a total output of 401.

Colburn was quicker than his contemporaries to understand the interdependence of various book-trade sectors: notably the mutual interest of the publisher, the lending library, and the opinion-forming journal. One of his more controversial initiatives was to secure these links by using his magazines to push his book to the library-owning purchaser and library-borrowing subscriber. In this early form of diversified book-trade operation (he was variously library-owner, retail bookseller, magazine proprietor, publisher), Colburn anticipated what is now called synergistic, or 'vertical', patterns of publishing.

Colburn anticipated other later publishing practices. His reliance on high pressure advertising is the clearest example. Promotion and publicity may not be the noblest division of publishing. But the twentieth-century book trade has universally followed Colburn in making it a main concern. As regards his more extravagant feats of 'puffing' (what is now called 'hype'), Colburn's main offence was to be ahead of his time and smarter than his competitors. He is well in line with the current trade wisdom that 'there's no such thing as a good book that doesn't sell'. Colburn's indifference to 'gentlemanly' codes of publishing behaviour is similarly in keeping with current thinking. Even his disdain for family 'house' publishing, in favour of opportunistic mergers, alliances and trade marriages of convenience (as with Bentley) fits in with contemporary business practice.

Although Colburn was principally a publisher of fiction, he was not exclusively so. He had strong subsidiary lines in popular travel and memoir literature (this last comprising biography, autobiography, and letters). Travel books comprise 141 of his total, memoirs 207. Together with the 527 fiction titles, these three categories dominate Colburn's output. Travel and memoirs were not one-season items, like fiction designed to sell fast. They had a longer life and provided backlist durability. Given his mix of books a case can be made for Colburn as a pioneer of 'General Trade Publishing'—that is, publishing based on books of the day (new novels) and slower moving items (usually non-fiction) which last for many seasons, or even years.

In short, it is time to see the Prince of Puffers as something much more than the publishing scamp of book-trade legend. A sure-footed pioneer, no less.

AFTERWORD:
'HENRY COLBURN, ESQ., THE EMINENT PUBLISHER'

Aside from the relentless focus on puffery, perhaps the thing that has most injured Henry Colburn's reputation over the years has been a widespread refusal to recognize him as an individual. If only he had been more like Bentley or Murray or some other publisher, his critics imply. If only he had been more gentlemanly, more literary, more morally scrupulous. If only he had been someone else, then, it seems, all would have been well. But, alas, he was determined to be Henry Colburn—and his reputation has suffered accordingly.

This book—rooted in Colburn's own business papers, letters and publications—has tried to take him on his own terms, even while acknowledging his place in the wider publishing world. We have jettisoned the 'if onlys' in order to attend to what was. It is precisely the kind of approach that Samuel Taylor Coleridge hoped others would take to his own story: 'By what I *have* effected, am I to be judged by my fellow men, what I could have done, is a matter for my own conscience'.[240]

What did Henry Colburn effect? When we run the

---

[240] *Biographia Literaria,* I 149–151.

numbers—he published so many novels, founded so many magazines, offered so many first-rate authors under his imprint—we reach one type of conclusion, by no means unimpressive. But Colburn was not a number-cruncher. He was an energetic entrepreneur, a shrewd risk-taker whose creativity happened to run in the profitable channels of capitalism. After ploughing all those qualities into the publishing industry for nearly half a century, Colburn reaped a harvest of accolades in the *Gentleman's Magazine*, whose November 1855 obituary piece was imprecise on dates and names but captured a true likeness of the man himself.

It is an important document because it is the most contemporary summary of his life and, crucially, it appears in a magazine not founded, published, owned, conducted or otherwise influenced by Colburn. Its anonymous writer was able to see—as we are now able to see—that 'the eminent Publisher' was in fact 'the principal publisher of novels and light literature of his time'. A simple sentence, it perfectly describes the success he achieved in his chosen arena without passing judgment on the value of that achievement. So, too, with the almost bland assertion that 'Mr. Colburn was unrivalled in the art of advertising his publications'. One might smile at the magazine's characterization of his puffery as 'frequent and judicious advertising', but these are plain statements based on established facts. Not surprisingly for a periodical publication, the *Gentleman's Magazine* devotes considerable attention to Colburn's founding any number of journals, 'most of them with great success.' Predating, as it does, the advent of Richard Bentley's vocal supporters Michael Sadleir and Royal Gettman, the obituary mentions Bentley only once and the Colburn and Bentley partnership only in passing.

While giving him full credit for what he had 'effected', the *Gentleman's Magazine* also mentions *how* Colburn effected it: after emerging from the shadows of Earle and

Morgan to run the Conduit Street establishment himself, he 'conducted the business with spirit and success.' Hard to quantify but continually in evidence, 'spirit' is just the right term for that exciting combination of zeal and chutzpah that Colburn brought not just to Conduit Street but to every one of his many different ventures. 'Bustling' is often used to describe him, but it never meant a harried racing to keep up with the pack; instead, it showed the vitality of a man who found the days too short to accommodate all of his new plans and ideas. F. Scott Fitzgerald wrote that 'Vitality shows in not only the ability to persist but the ability to start over'[241]—and how true that was of Henry Colburn. A man who was always prepared to risk failure as long as there was a fair chance of success, Colburn bounced back from financial losses, soured relationships and barbed criticisms that would have cowed lesser men. He had always a Plan B—or C, or D, if required. 'Like all who fundamentally believe in themselves he was rising to the occasion'.[242]

Colburn's spirit was indeed bolstered—if not positively driven—by his powerful self-belief. And this despite having family ties that had to be hidden rather than flaunted, and family money that set him up in business but was never in evidence again. A single man for most of his career, he had no wife or children to support him through the downturns and missteps. His confidence came from within. So innate was it that we easily take it for granted and overlook how extraordinary it was for the foremost publisher of fashionable novels to believe that he could also be the foremost publisher of military journals, or for a man who first studied the tastes of the reading public in the 1800s and 1810s to still be successfully divining them in the 1830s and 1840s. Yet Henry Colburn believed—*knew*—himself to be capable of such things and made them happen. Just

---

[241] *Notebooks*, cited in Columbia 678.
[242] Galsworthy, *In Chancery* 551.

as he knew that his puffery—however sneaky, however outlandish, however it enraged the critics—would sell books.

Can one wonder at the astonishing array of authors who submitted their work to him, cringe as they might at his wilder publicity schemes? The paper trail shows that Colburn often worked from 7:00 a.m. until midnight: smilingly greeting customers and authors, pursuing the absent by letter, planning the marketing for each of his titles individually, and forever turning over in his mind every little detail that might make or break a book. Of course authors wanted such a publisher busying himself over their precious manuscripts. And how much more important must he have been to those writers who relied on their pens to pay their bills? They had a publisher who was not just good at his job or suited to his work, but who loved every minute of it. That was the secret behind both his 'spirit' and his success.

APPENDIX ONE: BENTLEY'S UNPUBLISHED OBITUARY

This document was written sometime after Henry Colburn's funeral on 23 August 1855. Richard Bentley's grandson quoted extracts from it in his 1896 book, Some Leaves of the Past. What appears to be the sole surviving copy, consisting of proof sheets, is incomplete and ends abruptly. It is reprinted here courtesy of antiquarian Richard Ford of London.

August 16, 1855. This day died Henry Colburn, at his house in Bryanstone [sic] Square, in, I believe, his 71ˢᵗ year, although the coffin-plate which Horace read described him as aged 65. He had suffered more than a year before from a fistula, which had been successfully operated upon by Brodie; but about a month ago the disease returned, and after three days' intense suffering he sank under it. I went to his funeral in Kensal Green Cemetery, Thursday, August 23. It was conducted with more than ordinary form. Hearse with four horses, and two mourning coaches, and four private carriages. The coffin had gilt trappings.

Thus passed away one with whom formerly I was much connected, with whom I had much cruel and bitter law proceedings, who pursued me with bitter feeling to the last; but I thank God most heartily I did not sympathise with this feeling, for I had long ago forgiven him—forget the injuries he did me I cannot. If I live to have any leisure time, I will endeavour to put down some notice of this singular man, for his peculiarities were very amusing. I do not like, after all I have suffered from him, to think of him otherwise than calmly and impartially. In the character of his mind he was a *woman*, not regulated by manly judgment. No disparagement to the ladies, but that which is very amiable in them is scarcely so with men. When he took a notion or prejudice into his head it could not be removed; in that respect he considered his judgment infallible. In other matters the latest advice frequently prevailed. He never was in error; he had a most convenient way of shifting the burden from his own shoulders to those of others. That he possessed great tact is most true, and in conducting literary negotiations he had great adroitness, and skilfully availed himself of professional knowledge to induce those with whom he negotiated to consent to agreements which, if they had been duly instructed, they would not have done.

This was remarkably instanced in the case of Lord Normanby. He sold to Colburn his novel, [blank], for £600, £400 of which was to be paid at once, and the remaining £200 on 2nd edition. Lord Normanby, when I saw him afterwards, complained of Mr. Colburn's having misled him that he would get £600; this was to be regretted. He left the interest of £10,000 to his widow, with remainder to the children of Mr. Crosby [sic], her brother; £10,000 to Mr. Crosby, £100 to Campier, £800 to Mrs. Hurst. Whether this included all his property in copyright books, etc., I do not know, but should think not.

It was very painful to me that he should have died without our being reconciled, but, as I have previously said, my heart was at peace with him for many years. He kept a woman for some years who kept a library called Campbell's Library in Rathbone Place. This person he afterwards married. I shall never forget his coming to me one morning, with a singular expression of countenance, which made me anxious. I asked him what had happened— whether any ill-tidings of business caused him to look so oddly. After he had kept me waiting very anxious for a long time, he said he had a favour to ask me. I said I was sure he would not ask me to do anything which would not be a pleasure to me. At last he said he was going to be married. I said I was glad to hear it. He went on, 'and I wish you to give the bride away.' With all my heart,' said I. 'Well,' said he, 'on Thursday morning a coach will call for you, and bring you gloves [sic].' Accordingly, *this* lady was wedded to Harry Colburn at Marylebone Church, and I duly signed my name in the register.

The marriage was unfortunate. I suppose it is the fate of such marriages that it should be so. At any rate, Colburn did what I think was the part of a Christian and worthy member of society. This Mrs. Colburn took to drinking, and in her fits was very violent, and was a fruitful cause of trouble to the poor man. Finally she went to Boulogne, where she resided in apartments, and where, having abundance of cognac, she soon cut her way to death. He allowed her £300 a year there. His widow I have always heard well spoken of, as an agreeable woman, who rendered his latter days very comfortable.

I first became known to him through William Upcott, Librarian of the London Institution; I used to go down to Upcott to read the first proofs of 'Evelyn's Diary.' In 1819 dear Samuel and I went into business as printers, in Dorset Street, Salisbury Square, and in 1820 I first became known to Colburn. When the *New Monthly* was commenced under the editorship of Campbell we printed it, and afterwards became largely connected with Colburn. About 1825 a coolness came over our connection, in consequence of our pressing him a little for money, which we required. To renew this connection I proposed to him to transact any business for him in Paris during a visit I contemplated with two odd 'uns—Uncle Francis, 'dear child,' as Miss Swift calls him, 'of 70,' and Queer Tom the younger. These two I inveigled to Paris, believing they were only going to Canterbury to pay a visit to Mr. Read in Dame John.

On my return we gradually became more friendly, in consequence of my constant attention to him. So we went on; and in 1828–9 I learnt accidentally that Colburn was about to dispose of his business. He had spoken to Alderman Key, to the Magnays, and others. As our business with him was very important—about £3,000 to £3,500 a year—I did not like the idea of its going into hands adverse to us. Therefore I spoke to him about it. He was much pleased. I offered it to brother Samuel, who declined; then to brother Will, who also declined it. Then I said I would take it myself. Colburn wanted to associate others with me, which I declined. Then in September, 1829, I went into partnership with Colburn for three years; that is, to terminate in September, 1832, the conditions being that I was to pay on [the] first day of partnership £2,500 as my two-fifths of the partnership; Colburn to pay three-fifths. Any more money, if required, which Colburn had we would not be required to be furnished by Colburn at 5 per cent [sic].

So we begun [sic]. Colburn offered me copyright, and printed unpublished books to the amount of £10,000, for which he took credit at once. In the course of one year and a half of our partnership it clearly appeared that the major part of these books were comparatively worthless—certainly not worth half that they were valued at, and we soon began to want money. We drew monthly, I £50 and Colburn £75. Soon we had to raise money. Several schemes went wrong, 'The National Library' and the 'Juvenile Library' both failed. Then we had a sale at the Albion, where we realized from stock £2,700, for which it afterwards appeared we might have obtained from Tegg £4,000. Colburn mortgaged to me his one-third share of *Literary Gazette*, mortgaged to Key *New Monthly* and *United Service Journal*, sold his *Sunday Times* share, and his *Court Journal*.

All did not suffice. At the termination of our partnership I had lost the first sum of £2,500 and £1,300 more. Our agreement in the Deed of Partnership was that Colburn was to receive at the rate of two years' profits of the business as [t]he consideration for goodwill. This consideration he announced to be worth £5,000 a year; therefore he reckoned on receiving £10,000; now so far from profit there was a loss. And this loss he basely attributed to me, as a way of not paying for the business, forgetting that he himself always conducted it. 'Therefore,' he now said, 'the conditions not being fulfilled, of course I was to go about my business, as well as I could!' 'No,' said I; 'not if there is any redress from the law.' 'Well,' said he, 'you will find that what I say is correct. The law will not allow me to bind myself from going into business anywhere.' 'Then,' I said, 'you, who knew this, misled me. But I will see about that.'

Accordingly I went to Gregory, who corroborated what Colburn had said. Then I entered into arrangements with Colburn regarding Gregory,[243] this time to bind him fast, and he was bound, not to go into business within twenty miles of London, Edinburgh, or Dublin, and I paid him for this £3,500. But this could not bind him. So he threatened to go to Eton, twenty-one miles from London, and took a place. Then Upcott, his friend and *seemingly my* friend, came to me to endeavour to negotiate with me, for permission for Colburn to go into business. This I declined.

The same day I had a consultation with Mr. Knight Bruce, and when I found my agreement of no use in protecting me I was exceedingly angry with Gregory. On this Mr. Knight Bruce stopped me and said I was wrong in finding fault with Mr. Gregory, that it was impossible to frame any agreement for such a man. I said that it appeared to me that instead of protecting the right, law was made for the lawless. Mr. Knight Bruce observed that if a man chose so far to disregard the opinion of society as to do what Colburn was about to do, he could do it. 'Had

---

[243] This undoubtedly should read: 'I entered into arrangements with Gregory regarding Colburn'.

he offered me any money?' I said he had endeavoured to negotiate. 'For God's sake, sir, take his money—take his money!'

Heavy at heart I returned home, and did not sleep that night. I had refused to negotiate, and he could do as the rascal promised to do. In the morning, however, I received comfort. Upcott called again, and that time I hooked my trout. Affected not to desire it, said that if he would give me £10,000 for it it would not answer my purpose—that I did not buy it to recall it, etc. Finally, I agree[d] to let him go into business.

And he proceeded in the expectation that he would be able to crush me, as he had previously sought, but all in vain. In 1832, during our quarrel at the end of our partnership, he had intimated to several persons with whom we dealt—to Dickenson, the stationer, to Magnay, and others—that it would not be well to trust me. Then Dickenson declined, but I paid him for what I had, and so answered him. Magnay basely pressed me for the balance of account of Colburn and Bentley, for £1,600 goods had on the faith of our account and credit, and were shamed out of these proceedings by their own lawyers. For years afterwards I would have nothing to say to Magnay.

When Colburn first talked to me of his business he represented it to me as worth upwards of £5,000 a year, and I have his memorandum to me of this. In an article which appeared a day or two after his funeral in the *Morning Advertiser*,[244] he is said, 'despite a luckless partnership, to have died wealthy.' A more scoundrel-remark [...]

---

[244] This same article appeared as 'The Late Mr. Colburn' in the *Literary Gazette* on 1 September 1855, page 558.

APPENDIX TWO: COLBURN'S WILL

This document offers clarification of a few factual matters but like so many other things associated with Colburn, it is far more complicated than it initially seems and actually raises as many questions about his life and legacy as it answers. Henry Colburn drew up his will on 1 August 1854 with solicitors G. F. Hudson and C. Coupland of London—not otherwise known in Colburnian affairs.[245] After the brief preamble about his place of residence, it names Eliza as his sole executrix and her brother Malcolm Douglas Crosbie as her substitute should she predecease her husband. Like Colburn's solicitors, Malcolm enters Colburn's personal history with this will, in which he features prominently. Nothing is known about him before or after the date of this document. If it seems odd that a hitherto obscure relative should be suddenly elevated to the status of beneficiary and trustee of the publisher's estate, it must be remembered that Colburn had no known relatives of his own and Eliza seems to have had no one but Malcolm. The fact that Colburn's will is almost solely concerned with the Crosbies confirms suspicions that he had few personal ties outside of the publishing business.

---

[245] It is accessible via the National Archives (Public Records Office) as document PROB 11/2219, 445. Quotations are presented here are they appear in the original: *sans* punctuation.

Colburn's will does, however, mention a few people besides the Crosbie family and the first is indeed an acquaintance drawn from his business affairs. Immediately after the naming of his executor, Colburn begins distributing his largesse:

> I bequeath unto my friend Lavinia Hurst the wife of Daniel Hurst of Great Marlborough Street aforesaid Publisher as a mark of my esteem for her the sum of Five hundred pounds and for her sole and separate absolutely [sic] use independently of her said present or any future husband.

Because there is no previous indication of a close relationship—or indeed any relationship—between Colburn and his successor's wife, this special bequest comes as quite a surprise. Daniel Hurst had been his associate for so long that it was almost inevitable that Colburn would be on familiar terms with his wife but still unusual that he should remember her in his will with such a tidy sum. Just as intriguing as their relationship and the money is the clause keeping it out of Daniel Hurst's hands. It is tempting to imagine romantic explanations about Lavinia's secret life (and, indeed, Colburn's), but in the absence of any other evidence, one has to accept at face value Colburn's assertion that the gift is purely a mark of his 'esteem'.

Similar questions are posed by the next special bequest in Colburn's will, whereby he settles an annuity on 'Harriett Smith the wife of Philip Smith of Brook Street West Square South Lambeth'. The will states that the amount of the annuity shall be £80 as long as her mother Alice (surname illegible, unfortunately) is alive, but shall drop to £50 for the survivor 'after the death of either of them'. At no point does Philip Smith figure in the equation. Here again the absence of hard fact forces speculation as to who these people were and why Colburn bestowed money on them. There is some possibility of a romantic attachment to either Harriett or Alice, although if that were the case he might have been slightly more generous. A more prosaic possibility is that Harriett or Alice or both were servants in the Colburn household. This makes the sums seem reasonable (£80 annually would keep two working-class women comfortable but would have been insulting to someone of Lavinia Hurst's status) and could well explain why both women are mentioned in the will.

In the end, though, the simplest explanation for these bequests is that Colburn was just companionable with all of these women and wanted to ensure that they were well provided for when he was no longer around to look after them. This is in keeping with his generally good relations with women, his lack of other confidants and relatives to provide for in his will, and his known propensity for gift-giving. That Colburn should be friends with Lavinia, Harriet, and Alice and remember them in his will is, rather than unusual, almost to be expected.

After the bequests to these ladies, Colburn's will turns its full attention upon the most important lady in his life, destined to be his executor after his death, Eliza. Colburn bequeaths her £10,000 to be used to purchase annuities, which after her decease are to benefit Malcolm Crosbie's children: Maria, Fanny, Henry, Mary Alice, Arnold, and Eliza Ann. These children were, of course, the Colburns' nieces and nephews, and one cannot help noticing that the publisher and his wife have their own namesakes among them. Such strong familial bonds no doubt reflected genuine affection but must also have stemmed from the smallness of that family group. With no other claims upon his fortune, Colburn goes on to provide in his will another £10,000 to Malcolm himself, again to benefit the children after his demise. (The *Gentleman's Magazine* obituary makes a mistake here, claiming that the bequest was actually to Eliza's 'sister, the wife of Malcolm Douglas Crosbie';[246]

---

[246] P. 548.

apparently, no one thought to query why Eliza's brother-in-law shared her maiden name.)

Unfortunately for anyone attempting to read this will, matters are not set out as simply as they are here. Wills in general are not models of brevity, but Colburn's is a particularly painful example of a benefactor—or, perhaps that benefactor's solicitors—laboriously making provision for every possible eventuality. Thus, there are restrictions respecting the children's ages and the daughters' marital status, and endless contingency plans should one or some or all of the children die during Eliza or Malcolm's lifetimes. Then there is the naming of trustees and how one might go about resigning as a trustee or appointing a new one should an old one resign or die or 'go to reside beyond the Seas'. The document sprawls over six pages, each of them containing precisely fifty-seven closely written lines. This excess of detail may well be attributable to exceptionally zealous solicitors and clerks, but one would like to think that, after plenty of lawsuits over vague and poorly planned contracts, Henry Colburn had finally learned to demand a precise and unchallengeable legal document.

Almost buried beneath repetitious jargon and interminable clauses lies one last bequest, with some very interesting and even problematic caveats attached. To appreciate fully the situation Colburn constructed, it is necessary to quote at length:

> And as to all that my Leasehold Messuage or [illegible] house in which I now reside situate in Bryanstone Square aforesaid and all my Copyrights and ALL THE REST AND RESIDUE OF MY PROPERTY ESTATE AND EFFECTS whether [illegible] or personal or whatsoever and wheresoever and including what may be undisposed of of my said property in the improbable event of none of the said children of the said Malcolm Douglas Crosbie acquiring a vested Interest in their said Legacies or bequests I give devise and bequeath the said

unto my said wife for her own sole and separate absolute use and benefit Provided always that in case my wife shall die in my lifetime then I devise and bequeath my said Leasehold Messuage [illegible] house copyrights and all other my said residuary property estate and effects unto the said Malcolm Douglas Crosbie his heirs executors administrators and assigns according to the nature and quality thereof respectively [illegible] that he or they be and shall with all convenient speed after my decease sell all and convert into money all the said Leaseholds copyrights and other residuary personal Estate and effects[.]

The unfortunate illegibilities obfuscate matters, but it seems that Eliza was to inherit his property to do with as she pleases, while Malcolm and his heirs, should they inherit, would be forced to convert the property into ready cash.

Why Colburn would make such a proviso is yet another question without a definite answer. The simplest explanation may be that it is only possible to fairly divide an inheritance between six children and their father once that inheritance is liquidated. This would certainly preclude any arguing over who got the Maclise painting, whether to sell the house, and so on. The publisher managed to introduce an amusing note into the legalistic proceedings at this point—though unintentionally—by directing Malcolm and his heirs to spend whatever amount they deem 'reasonable for promoting and facilitating such Sale or Sales'. Only Colburn would contrive to advertise from beyond the grave.

Though a carefully constructed document, his will is not without its flaws, and the chief one appears in relation to the notable matter of his copyrights. In the long quotation above, these copyrights are included in the property that Eliza inherits outright and that Malcolm must sell. Nevertheless, they are mentioned later, after the advertising proviso, as a separate entity exempt from the big property sale: 'as to my Copyrights the said Malcolm Douglas Crosbie shall have full discretion and authority to sell or to retain and publish the same as he shall think best'. Because Eliza survived her husband, and her brother never inherited, these conflicting clauses were never subjected to legal scrutiny. The latter clause does, however, imply that Colburn trusted Malcolm to put his copyrights to good use, just as he trusted Eliza. What actually happened to these copyrights—involving Charles Dickens and Eliza Colburn's second husband—is yet another enigmatic episode in Colburn's uncertain history.

APPENDIX THREE: THE COLBURN-BENTLEY INDENTURE

Richard Bentley signed an Indenture with Henry Colburn on 3 June 1829 that was to go into effect on 31 August of that year.[247] Financially, the crux of the matter was an apportioning of three-fifths for Colburn and two-fifths for Bentley, which represented the division of profits (Article 3), debts (Article 10), and expenses (Article 7). In regard to the latter, Bentley was liable for sums totalling no more than £2,500, after which point Colburn was to pay on his behalf. That £2,500 thus became the price of Bentley's partnership.

The Indenture allowed Bentley to reside in the part of the house on New Burlington Street not taken up by the business and to have the lease transferred to his name after the dissolution of the partnership. The Indenture gave Colburn the right of entry to the premises whenever he desired it, 'without being bound to be there more than he shall think proper' (Article 5). The implication that Colburn would be distancing himself from the day-to-day operations of the firm—largely to accommodate his health problems, as his letters reveal—was subsequently made explicit, as was Bentley's subjection to Colburn:

---

[247] It is among the Bentley Papers in the British Library, Add.MS.46632A, 3–13.

the said Richard Bentley shall & will during the said copartnership take upon himself all the active part of the said Business & all the labor [sic] & trouble of carrying on & conducting the same in a manner subject to the approbation of the said Henry Colburn & for that purpose shall give up all his time & attention to the same & shall exert himself with due care & diligence to manage & promote the same to the best of his judgment & ability. (Article 6)

The bookkeeping (Article 8) and even the annual stocktaking and division of profits (Article 16) fell to Bentley. The Indenture made clear that the permission of both partners was necessary for most business dealings, but Colburn's periodicals were entirely exempt from the agreement—they were to remain his alone, both during and after the partnership. To all appearances, a semi-retirement as the distant proprietor of a few popular journals awaited Henry Colburn in 1832.

Looking ahead to that time, the Indenture set a price on Colburn's interest in the firm: Bentley was to pay him £10,000 for the business if that amount was approximately equal to two-thirds of the total value of the business (Article 17). The valuation was to include the profits made during the three years of the partnership, unsold stock, and copyrights—but did not include Colburn's periodicals or any of the stock and copyrights he owned prior to the inception of the partnership on 31 August 1829, which remained entirely in his possession (Article 24). If two-thirds of the firm's value was greater than £10,000, Bentley was to increase his payment accordingly; if the value was less than £10,000 or if the partners disagreed over the valuation, they were each to select an 'indifferent person', both of whom would then choose an 'umpire' to arbitrate the matter (Articles 30 & 32).

At first sight £10,000 looks like a reasonable price for such an established and successful business, but Articles

20 through 22 of the Indenture show that this was no bargain. All that money bought Bentley was the lease on the premises (an ongoing expense of £210 per year) and, as subsequent documents put it, Henry Colburn's 'good will'. It did not include Colburn's three-fifths interest in the firm's jointly held copyrights and unsold stock—though the Indenture gave Bentley first option to buy them and thoughtfully provided a timetable for the appropriate payments to Colburn, using his two-fifths share of the partnership's holdings as 'collateral security' (Article 22).

While the Indenture demanded a great deal of cash from Bentley, it also held out a great promise that must have comforted him as he toiled for three years at running another man's business: in the end, not only would he be an independent operator, but he also would have no direct competition. A significant part of Colburn's success stemmed from the fact that he had constructed a niche market all his own, based around fashionable novels—and after 31 August 1832, it would all be Bentley's. Article 26 of the Indenture made sure of this:

> the said Henry Colburn shall engage & covenant not to purchase for separate publication or publish without the consent of the said Richard Bentley any new Book or Work of any person or persons whomsoever on his own private or separate acct nor shall not nor will at any time hereafter print or publish or be concerned or engaged in the printing or publishing of any Books Works Copyrights or publications or in any manner use exercise or carry on the Trade or Business of a Bookseller or Publisher or enter into or be engaged or interested in any literary Speculations of what nature or kind soever Save as hereinafter next mentioned.

The exceptions were no surprise: Colburn could carry on with his journals and sell and reprint all of his pre-1829 holdings at will; most of the periodicals and all of the books had to be published via Bentley (at a commission of two percent), which would ensure a steady income and serve as a sign of Colburn's continuing good will. Bentley also had first option to buy the journals when Colburn decided to retire altogether.

APPENDIX FOUR: A COLBURN CHRONOLOGY

c.1784 Born—day, place, and parents unknown

c.1800 Works as assistant to bookseller William Earle at 47 Albemarle Street

1806 Publishes first books from the Public Library at 48-50 Conduit Street

c.1812 Assumes full control of Conduit Street library

1814 Founds the *New Monthly Magazine*—first issue appears on 1 February

1817 Founds the *Literary Gazette*—first issue appears on 25 January

c.1820 Relinquishes control of Conduit Street library to Saunders and Otley but maintains publishing business on the premises; Eliza Ann Crosbie born

1823–24 Relinquishes Conduit Street premises to Saunders and Otley; sets up publishing business at 8 New Burlington Street

1828 Founds the *Athenaeum* in January but sells out in May

1829 Founds the *Court Journal* and the *United Service Journal;* Bentley buys a partnership in Colburn's firm, effective 31 August

1830 Weds Mary Campbell but is widowed the following year—no children

1832 Goes into semi-retirement managing his periodicals and old copyrights; Bentley controls the New Burlington

Street firm from 1 September

1836 Establishes firm in Windsor before agreeing to terms with Bentley; returns to London and establishes new firm at 13 Great Marlborough Street

1841 Marries Eliza Ann Crosbie—no children; sells his share of the *Literary Gazette* to William Jerdan

1845 Sells the *New Monthly Magazine* to William Harrison Ainsworth

1852–53 Retires; sells firm to Hurst and Blackett

1855 Dies in his home at 14 Bryanston Square on 16 August; buried at Kensal Green Cemetery on 23 August

1856 Eliza Colburn marries John Forster on 24 September

1857 Colburn's stock and copyrights are auctioned on 26 May

1894 Eliza Forster dies and is buried in Kensal Green Cemetery next to John Forster

BIBLIOGRAPHY
MANUSCRIPT MATERIALS

Bentley, Richard. Diaries, 1859–1871. Bentley Papers. University of Illinois at Urbana-Champaign.

—. Obituary of Henry Colburn, with other miscellaneous papers. Private collection of Richard Ford.

—. Papers. British Library.

Bishops' Transcripts, Entry 24557. London Metropolitan Archives.

Colburn, Henry. Last Will and Testament. Public Record Office: PROB 11/2219, Image 445.

Faculty Office Marriage Licence Allegation 0243679. Lambeth Palace, London.

Forster, John. Papers. National Art Library, Victoria and Albert Museum.

Hughenden (Benjamin Disraeli) Papers. Bodleian Library, Oxford University.

Sadleir, Michael. Papers. Manuscripts Department, Wilson Library, University of North Carolina at Chapel Hill.

Vicar-General Marriage Licence Allegation 66663. Lambeth Palace, London.

COLBURN PERIODICALS

Court Journal. 1829–30.

Literary Gazette. 1817–42.

New British Theatre. 1814–1815.
New Monthly Magazine and Humourist. 1837–45.
New Monthly Magazine and Literary Journal. 1821–37. *New Monthly Magazine and Universal Register.* 1814–21. *Quarterly Journal of Science and the Arts.* 1827–29. *United Service Journal.* 1829–53.

WORKS CITED

Adburgham, Alison. *Silver Fork Society: Fashionable Life and Literature from 1814 to 1840.* London: Constable, 1983.

Barnes, James J. *Free Trade in Books: A Study of the London Book Trade Since 1800.* Oxford: Clarendon, 1964.

Beattie, William. *The Life and Letters of Thomas Campbell.* 3 vols. London: Moxon, 1849.

Bentley, Richard. *Some Leaves from the Past, Swept Together by R. B.* Privately printed, 1896.

Blake, Robert. *Disraeli.* London: Eyre & Spottiswoode, 1966.

Brown, Philip A. H. *London Publishers and Printers c.1800–1870.* London: British Library, 1982.

Byron, George Gordon, Lord. *Byron's Letters and Journals.* Ed. Leslie A. Marchand. 12 vols. London: Murray, 1973–1982.

Carpenter, Humphrey. *The Seven Lives of John Murray: The Story of a Publishing Dynasty.* London, 2008.

Chapman, John. *Cheap Books and How to Get Them.* London: 1852.

Chilcott, Tim. *A Publisher and His Circle: The Life and Work of John Taylor, Keats's Publisher.* London: Routledge & Kegan Paul, 1972.

Coleridge, Samuel Taylor. *Biographia Literaria.* 1817. Ed. J. Shawcross. 2 vols. London: OUP, 1907.

Columbia Dictionary of Quotations. Ed. Robert Andrews. NY: Columbia UP, 1993.

Crompton, Louis. *Byron and Greek Love: Homophobia in Nineteenth-Century England.* London: Faber & Faber, 1985.

Curwen, Henry. *A History of Booksellers: The Old and the*

New. London: Chatto & Windus, 1873.

Dibdin, T. F. *Bibliophobia: Remarks on the Present Languid and Depressed State of Literature and the Book Trade*. London: 1832.

Dickens, Charles. *The Letters of Charles Dickens*. Pilgrim Edition. Madeline House, Graham Storey, and Kathleen Tillotson, gen. eds. 12 vols. Oxford: Clarendon, 1965–2002.

Dictionary of National Biography. Ed. Leslie Stephen and Sidney Lee. 22 vols. London: Smith, Elder, 1908–09.

Disraeli, Benjamin. *Letters*. 6 vols. Toronto: Univ. of Toronto Press, 1982–97.

—. *The Young Duke*. 1831. London: Longmans, 1881.

'The Dominie's Legacy'. *Fraser's Magazine* 1 (Apr 1830): 318–335.

Downey, Edmund. *Charles Lever: His Life in His Letters*. London: 1906.

Ellis, S. M. *William Harrison Ainsworth and His Friends*. London: 1911.

The English Catalogue of Books, 1801–1836. London, 1914.

—. *The English Catalogue, 1835–1862*. London: 1864.

Erickson, Lee, ed. *The Economy of Literary Form: English Literature and the Industrialization of Publishing, 1800–1850*. Baltimore: Johns Hopkins UP, 1996.

Galsworthy, John. *In Chancery*. 1920. *The Forsyte Saga*. NY: Touchstone, 2004.

Gautier, Maurice-Paul. *Captain Frederick Marryat*. Paris: Didier, 1973.

Gettmann, Royal A. *A Victorian Publisher: A Study of the Bentley Papers*. Cambridge: Cambridge UP, 1960.

Gibson, M. *Dracula and the Eastern Question: British and French Vampire Narratives of the Nineteenth-Century Near East*. New York: 2006.

Grill, Neil Gilbert. 'The *New Monthly Magazine:* 1814–21'. Ph.D. diss., New York University, 1970.

Hall, S. C. *Retrospect of a Long Life*. 2 vols. London: Bentley, 1883.

Higgins, David. 'The *New Monthly Magazine*'. *The Literary Encyclopedia*. First published 22 October 2006. [http://www.litencyc.com/php/stopics.php?rec=true&UID=1682, accessed 22 May 2017.]

James, Elizabeth F., ed. *Macmillan: A Publishing Tradition, 1843–1970*. London: Palgrave, 2002.

Jerman, Bernard R. 'The Production of Disraeli's Trilogy.' *PBSA* 58 (1964): 239–51.

—. *The Young Disraeli*. Princeton, NJ: Princeton UP, 1960.

Jones, Linda B. 'The *New Monthly Magazine, 1821–1830*'. Ph.D. diss., University of Colorado, 1970.

Macdonald, D. L. *Poor Polidori*. Toronto: University of Toronto Press, 1991.

Maginn, William. *Whitehall; or, The Days of George IV*. London: Marsh, 1827.

Martineau, Harriet. *Autobiography*. Ed. Maria Weston Chapman. 2 vols. Boston: 1878.

Melnyk, Veronica. "'Half fashion and half passion': The Life of Publisher Henry Colburn". Ph.D. thesis, University of Birmingham. 2002, http://etheses.bham.ac.uk/163/.

'Mr. Edward Lytton Bulwer's Novels'. *Fraser's Magazine* 1 (June 1830): 509–532.

Mumby, Frank A. *Publishing and Bookselling: A History from the Earliest Times to the Present Day*. London: Cape, 1930.

'Noctes Ambrosianae'. *Blackwood's Edinburgh Magazine* 20 (July 1826): 90–109, (Nov 1826): 770–792.

'The Novels of the Season'. *Fraser's Magazine* 3 (Feb 1831): 95–113.

'Obituary—Henry Colburn'. *Gentleman's Magazine*, n.s., 44 (Nov 1855): 547–548.

Oliphant, Margaret. *Annals of a Publishing House: William Blackwood and His Sons, Their Magazines and Friends*. 2 vols. Edinburgh: Blackwood, 1897.

Patmore, P. G. *My Friends and Acquaintance*. 3 vols. London: Saunders & Otley, 1854.

Redding, Cyrus. *Fifty Years' Recollections, Literary and Personal*. 3 vols. London: Skeet, 1858.

—. *Literary Reminiscences and Memoirs of Thomas Campbell*. 2 vols. London: Skeet, 1860.

—. *Yesterday and Today*. 3 vols. London: Newby, 1863.

Reid, J. C. *Thomas Hood*. London: 1963.

Renton, Richard. *John Forster and His Friendships*. London: Chapman & Hall, 1912.

Ridley, Jane. *The Young Disraeli, 1804–1846*. London: Sinclair-Stevenson, 1996.

Rieger, James. 'Dr. Polidori and the Genesis of *Frankenstein*'. *Studies in English Literature 1500–1900* (Winter 1963): pages?

Rollins, Hyder E. 'Letters of Horace Smith to His Publisher Colburn'. *Harvard Library Bulletin* 3 (autumn 1949): 359–370.

Rosa, Matthew W. *The Silver-Fork School: Novels of Fashion Preceding Vanity Fair*. 1936. Columbia University Studies in English and Comparative Literature, no. 123. Port Washington, NY: Kennikat, 1964.

Rossetti, William Michael ed. *The Diary of Dr. John William Polidori, 1816, relating to Byron, Shelley, etc.* New York: 2009.

Sadleir, Michael. *Bulwer and His Wife: A Panorama*. London: Constable, 1933.

—. *Nineteenth-Century Fiction: A Bibliographical Record Based on His Own Collection*. 2 vols. Cambridge: Cambridge UP, 1951.

Shelley, Mary Wollstonecraft. *Letters*. Ed. Betty T. Bennett. Baltimore: 1980.

Smiles, Samuel, *A Publisher and his Friends*. 2 vols. London: 1891.

Stevenson, Lionel. *The Wild Irish Girl*. London: 1936.

Stott, Andrew McConnell. 'The Poet, the Physician and the Birth of the Modern Vampire'. https://publicdomainreview.org/2014/10/16/the-poet-the-physician-and-the-birth-of-the-modern-vampire/

Sutherland, John. 'The British Book Trade and the Crash of 1826'. *The Library*, 6th ser., 9 (1987): 148–161.

—. 'Henry Colburn, Publisher'. *Publishing History* 19 (1986): 59–84.

—. *The Life of Sir Walter Scott.* London: 1994.

—. *Victorian Fiction: Writers, Publishers, Readers.* Basingstoke: Macmillan, 1995.

Thackeray, William M. *The History of Pendennis.* 1848–50. Ed. John Sutherland. World's Classics. Oxford: Oxford UP, 1999.

Thrall, Miriam M. H. *Rebellious Fraser's.* Columbia University Studies in English and Comparative Literature, no. 117. New York: Columbia UP, 1934.

'Town and Table Talk on Literature, Art, Etc.' *Illustrated London News* (25 Aug 1855): 231.

Tucker, Albert. 'Military'. In *Victorian Periodicals and Victorian Society,* ed. J. Don Vann and Rosemary T. VanArsdel. Aldershot: Scolar, 1994.

Wilson, Cheryl A. *Fashioning the Silver Fork Novel.* London: Pickering & Chatto, 2012.

Wilson, Frances, ed. *Byromania: Portraits of the Artist in Nineteenth- and Twentieth-Century Culture.* London: Macmillan, 1999.

Wu, Duncan. *William Hazlitt: The First Modern Man.* Oxford: OUP, 2008.

THE AUTHORS

John Sutherland is the Lord Northcliffe Emeritus Professor at University College, London. In a long scholarly career one of his main areas of interest has been the history of Victorian publishing. Henry Colburn has long been an object of fascination to him.

Veronica Melnyk earned degrees from DePaul University in Chicago and the University of Birmingham, where she completed her doctoral thesis on Henry Colburn. She is now the Prioress of the Olivetan Benedictine Sisters of Jonesboro, Arkansas, and is known in religious life as Sister Johanna Marie.

ACKNOWLEDGEMENTS

The drawing of Henry Colburn which forms the frontispiece is the only known portrait of him, and we are grateful to the owner of the drawing, Sibylla Flower, for permission to print it here. Collection: Sibylla Jane Flower: 'Portrait of Henry Colburn', black crayon heightened with red, 270 x 200mm, signed and dated by Count D'Orsay, 'd'Orsay fecit 18.July 1845', also signed by Colburn in ink.

The two original autograph letters signed by Henry Colburn and the photographs of some of Colburn's publications are from original copies in The John Spiers Collection of Victorian and Edwardian Fiction.

The illustrations of some of Colburn's authors are reproduced from John Sutherland's copy of *The Maclise portrait-gallery of illustrious literary characters, with memoirs biographical, critical, bibliographical, and anecdotal illustrative of the literature of the former half of the present century* (London, Chatto & Windus, 1883).

INDEX

www.ingramcontent.com/pod-product-compliance
Lightning Source LLC
Chambersburg PA
CBHW060310100426
42812CB00003B/729